MATRON
AT WAR

MATRON
AT WAR

THE STORY OF KATY BEAUFOY
(1869 – 1918)

Erica Nadin-Snelling

BREWIN BOOKS

BREWIN BOOKS
56 Alcester Road,
Studley,
Warwickshire,
B80 7LG
www.brewinbooks.com

Published by Brewin Books 2014

A CIP catalogue record for this book is available from the British Library.

ISBN: 978-1-85858-520-8

Printed and bound in Great Britain
by 4edge Ltd.

CONTENTS

Katy's Great Nieces, from left: Clair, Erica, Gill and Sue.

MATRON AT WAR

THE STORY OF KATY BEAUFOY (1869 – 1918)

THE STORY INCLUDES HER DIARY FROM 10TH MAY 1915 TO 9TH SEPTEMBER 1917, A FASCINATING ACCOUNT OF HER SERVICE AS SISTER AND MATRON IN THE GREAT WAR, THE FATE OF THE GLENART CASTLE AND KATE'S FAMILY MEMBERS IN THE FIRST WORLD WAR

The diary has been faithfully reproduced with abbreviations and spellings as written, gaps where she meant to add a name but never had time and part text July – September 1916 where the pages were torn.

It was originally inaugurated by, Margaret Gillian Morgan, and transcribed to book format by Joyce and Michael Harrison, being finally produced by Erica Nadin-Snelling (née Beaufoy) and her daughter Deborah Sullivan. This is all possible thanks to Sue Wood who has carefully conserved and made available the diary and medals. The author would also like to thank Claire Burley for contributing Katy's letter from the Boer War.

MEDALS & AWARDS

ST. BARNABUS HOSPITAL, LONDON (for services to nursing) right. QUEEN OF ITALY'S MEDAL (for services to nursing) left.

SOUTH AFRICAN WAR MEDAL (Boer War).

BRONZE DEATH PLAQUE (Dead Woman's Penny): (Note – the correct spelling is KATY not KATE).

PRINCESS CHRISTIAN'S ARMY NURSING SERVICE.

1915 STAR, VICTORY MEDAL & GREAT WAR MEDAL (popularly known as Pip, Squeak & Wilfred).

PAGE OF ORIGINAL DIARY
(reproduced here at full size)

So fortunate that Sue Wood kept this diary as it is almost illegible and would have been discarded by many!

All photographs that appear in this book courtesy of Sue Wood, Erica Nadin-Snelling, Gill Morgan, Joyce & Michael Harrison.

THE BEAUFOY FAMILY TREE

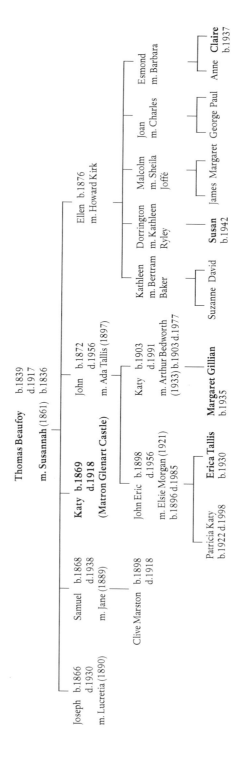

Thomas Beaufoy b.1839 d.1917
m. Susannah (1861) b.1836

Joseph b.1866 d.1930
m. Lucretia (1890)

Samuel b.1868 d.1938
m. Jane (1889)

Katy b.1869 d.1918
(Matron Glenart Castle)

John b.1872 d.1956
m. Ada Tallis (1897)

Ellen b.1876
m. Howard Kirk

Clive Marston b.1898 d.1918

John Eric b.1898 d.1956
m. Elsie Morgan (1921) b.1896 d.1985

Katy b.1903 d.1991
m. Arthur Bedworth (1933) b.1903 d.1977

Kathleen m. Bertram Baker

Dorrington m. Kathleen Ryley

Malcolm m. Sheila Joffé

Joan m. Charles

Esmond m. Barbara

Patricia Katy b.1922 d.1998

Erica Tallis b.1930

Margaret Gillian b.1935

Suzanne David

Susan b.1942

James Margaret George Paul

Anne Claire b.1937

x

1. INTRODUCTION

By Gill Morgan

It was a gloriously warm spring morning in May 2000. I was in the confines of the sad but hauntingly beautiful surroundings of the Commonwealth War Graves Commission cemetery located at Vielle Chapelle in Northern France. My reason for being in this village of the dead had been to visit the grave of Clive Marston Beaufoy; Clive came from my Mother's side of the family and had been killed in action fighting as an officer with the Royal Warwickshire Regiment on September 25th 1918.

As I prepared to leave I fell in to step with my guide for the pilgrimage, Michael Harrison. The stark reminders of the cost of failed diplomacy were all around us so it was only natural that thoughts turned to families and what might have been. Memories came tumbling back of a story my Mother used to tell. The half-forgotten tale related how Clive's auntie, Katy Beaufoy, had died when the ship in which she was serving had been torpedoed off the coast of Ireland during the Great War. In the short time that it took to reach our coach I had imparted the story as I knew it to Michael who promised to "look into it" for me.

May stretched in to June without word, when one day out of the blue, my former guide telephoned to say that information about Katy had come to light. Great Auntie Katy had been lost when His Majesty's Hospital Ship, Glenart Castle, was torpedoed off 'Lundy Island' on February 26th 1918. Katy, who was serving as Matron in the ship and the other six female nurses, had been drowned. We were later able to obtain a fix on the ship's position as 20 miles WSW of Hartland Point in North Devon. The wreck lies 31 fathoms deep and at the time (June 2000) had not been dived.

By nature I am inquisitive and so are my friends. With a story as powerful as this it was inevitable that the matter would have to be taken further. The box had been opened and now we could not close it again. Contact was established with Ilfracombe Sub Aqua Club and in particular, Keith Denby, who by coincidence had become greatly interested in the ship at the same time as ourselves. Knowing their way around the maritime agencies and archives the Club discovered that the ship and her true position had been identified during a recent survey of the seabed. This in their unstinting and kindly way they passed on to us.

A mighty yet benign force seemed to be at work as the story unfolded. Doors to knowledge of the subject swung open when an old neighbour told me of two cousins (Claire Burley and Sue Wood) that I never knew I had. At our first meeting Sue produced Katy's diary, medals, photographs and her 'Dead Woman's Penny'.

A long but inspiring journey had begun; the trail would lead to the Mediterranean taking in the West Country and Southampton. People who are as far apart in geographical terms as Canada and Australia would be drawn into the story. I feel that I now know Great Auntie Katy and for the sake of her memory and those who sailed with her this journey had to be undertaken. It is my sincere wish that you join me in this exploration wherever it might lead.

FOR THOSE IN PERIL ON THE SEA

2. FAMILY PHOTOGRAPHS
THE BEAUFOY FAMILY

Back row left to right – Lucretia, Joseph, John, Katy, Ellen, (brother Sam was in Ceylon), (Louie), (Joe). Front row – Susannah & Thomas. Photograph taken in Joseph's home at 4 Hollyfield Road, Sutton Coldfield – now demolished.

Thomas Beaufoy and Susannah née Marston, circa 1910.

The Clock given to Thomas Beaufoy on his retirement from the Royal Mail.

Tallis family at The Beeches, Solihull. Katy is the young girl seated at the front.

Clive Marston Beaufoy (left) K.I.A. Sept 1918. John Eric Beaufoy.

Katy and John Eric Beaufoy 2.7.1917.

3. THE EARLY YEARS

Letter from The Boer War

Katy Beaufoy came into this world on December 20th 1869, the third of five children. Her delighted parents were Susannah (nee Marston) and Thomas. There were two elder brothers Joseph and Samuel and Katy was succeeded by another brother John and a final sister Ellen (known to Katy as Sissy). The couple had married at the church of St. Paul, Polesworth, on October 27th 1861.

Katie had inherited her sense of purpose and diligence from her parents, Thomas, whose father died when he was 9 years old became a silk weaver at the age of 11 eventually marrying the girl next door (Susannah). Education was not compulsory and Thomas was self taught, the Churches and Sunday schools were a very important fund of education prior to the Education Act. Thomas never lost his love for reading and his bequeath of books were mentioned in his will. The family were brought up with a respect and love of learning. Thomas moved to Birmingham after the start of the national postal service starting as a temporary letter carrier at 18 shillings a week! Eventually rising to superintendent of Birmingham postal services which at that time employed over 1000 men.

1869 was the thirty-second year of the reign of Queen Victoria. Great Britain, a tiny offshore island, had amassed the largest empire the world had ever known. The "Pax Britannica" was in reality a global trading conglomerate, the head office of which was our tiny island refuge. The Empire did and still does to this day have its critics but the Victorians were virtually 100% intensely proud of their country and its achievements.

This then was Katy's world; vast areas of the planet were the Victorians' fiefdom, policed by a diminutive army with its worldwide shipping routes in the constant care of the Royal Navy. The goods and wealth flowed in all directions and it seemed as if it would all go on forever. Not that the world was perfect, it never was and never will be. To claim that it could be otherwise is a falsehood practised by the political classes of many countries. The enormous treasure generated by the Empire did not trickle down to everyone; for many people emigration was the only answer. Australia, New Zealand, Canada and South Africa were the favourite destinations for those who wished to escape the clutches of unemployment and a damp climate.

Following his long employment after receiving the conventional 'clock' Thomas, Susannah and Katie moved to "South View", a house situated on Whitehouse Common near the town of Sutton Coldfield. Katy herself travelled into the City of "1000 Trades" from an early age as we know from surviving documents that she received her early education at "St. Clement's, Birmingham". Her time was that of gaslights, steam locomotives, horses and of course strict and inviolable class divisions. As an aside, to illustrate the last point, we have two very similar roads of Victorian houses in a part of Solihull which, to us, look much the same. In the heyday of railway commuter house building, we are told that the residents of the two roads never spoke. The reason for this social exclusion? One road was slightly more expensive than the other. Perhaps that's one reason why the Victorians are so much of an enigma to us; they would go out of their way to build fences rather than bridges and yet the country was being engulfed in a tidal wave of religious revival that preached "Love Thy Neighbour".

Unfortunately, we know little of Katy's childhood. She next appears in records when in 1893 she was successful in her application for the post of trainee nurse at the Royal Devon and Exeter Hospital. That Katy was a diligent student can be evinced by the fact that just three years later, from December 1st 1896, she had been made Sister In Charge of the Operating Theatre. Two and a half years later, in 1898, she became Sister In Charge of thirty-three beds on the Men's Medical Ward, relinquishing this position on New Year's Eve, 1898. Never one to sit back, New Year's Day found her appointed as Matron of the eighty-bed Exeter Fever Hospital. It was here that Katy faced her greatest test so far. An epidemic of the deadly enteric fever broke out in the surrounding district and for months she never had less than fifty cases of this virulent disease to cope with.

My own view of Katy's vocation at the time of the above-mentioned epidemic leads me to use the metaphor: she was in the 'front line trenches' of medical care. The main weapons in her armoury with which to fight the disease were no more than the strictest of hygiene regimes and the obedience and self-discipline of her staff. Enteric fever and typhoid share the same ugly traits. They begin life wherever water is contaminated or sewage treatment is poor to non-existent. Any food handled by a carrier of the disease or touched by a fly from an infected area can transmit the potentially fatal illness. The victim's temperature reaches 105 accompanied by chronic bouts of vomiting and diarrhoea. If the patient were to survive he or she could look forward to four weeks of these conditions. No drugs or anti-biotics were available at the time – only the Nursing Sisters' courage and unremitting insistence on hygiene and the administration of fluids and salt, to replace those lost, stood between the victim and the local graveyard. The fluids and salt had to be administered by mouth, as it was not until WW2 that safe intravenous drips came into use. If we look at the risk of infection involved in the care of these patients: one moment of forgetfulness on the part of an exhausted Sister could have easily led to that person changing roles and becoming a patient herself. They all, each and every one of them, deserved some form of recognition by the State. Each day of duty during that dreadful four-month period, when the disease marched rampant through parts of the West Country, Katy and her brave colleagues risked their lives. August 2nd 1900 saw Katy relinquish her position at Exeter.

Times were changing and cracks began to appear in the cohesion of the Empire. Twenty years before in the early 1880s, the cultures of Britain and Holland had clashed in South Africa. Now war had flared once more in the Transvaal and the Orange Free State. The Boer farmers with the mischievous backing of some Europeans had taken the road to independence. Britain's tiny standing Army was in no condition to take on the hard-bitten farmers who knew every stone and bush in the country. Added to that, the Boers were legendary in their mobility on the battlefield. Using small, rugged ponies they formed themselves into "Commandos" who appeared seemingly from nowhere and as quickly disappeared into the bush, leaving little or no trace of their coming. Outclassed and out manoeuvred, the British Army had lost the initiative; it was now their enemy that dictated the course of the War. In a desperate attempt to regain control of events there occurred perhaps the saddest chapter in the history of our Armies. Put bluntly, to reduce the will of the farmers to fight, their wives and children were rounded up and interned in camps where 28,000 victims died of starvation. In an eerie prophecy of things to come these vile establishments became known as "Concentration Camps". The British public through the work of a lady, Emily Hobhouse, knew the existence of the camps. Through Emily, reports reached London and the national press. The ensuing public outcry against the barbarous treatment of the Boer families caused a tide of revulsion to sweep the country. To add to the manifold problems faced by the Army Staff, soldiers were being overcome by disease at an alarming rate and with little hope of recovery given the limited means at the disposal of the medical services.

Waiting in the wings, as events in South Africa reached a new low, was one Alexandra Caroline Mary Charlotte Louise Julia, otherwise known as Queen Alexandra. The Queen who was the mother of the future King George V persuaded Maude McCarthy, an expert nurse, to take five other Sisters with her to South Africa to turn around the tottering medical organisation. Great things were achieved by this small but intrepid group of ladies and on their return to the UK in 1902 the body known as Queen Alexandra's Imperial Military Nursing Service Reserve was founded. The organisation still exists today, administering to the needs of sick and injured soldiers.

As always our dear Katy could not hold back when the need for nurses was greatest. She volunteered her services to help in South Africa. In a letter home (sent during the **Boer War**) she describes a snapshot of the life she was leading within the boom of the guns and the following is in Katy's own words: -

18 General Hospital
Charlestown
Natal
8 – 3 – 02
3.15am.

Dear Sis,

I intended to write to you in time for yesterday's mail, but could not; I have been too busy. I have only one more night on night duty. I am so glad as we have had such a very trying time, the weather has been frightfully bad, only had two fine nights & it is so trying to walk on this slippy, slanting ground, all the while stepping across the trenches round the tents. Sunday night last beat all, rain tumbling down, wind blowing strong & cold & busiest night. I was out in it nearly the whole night, sat down in the duty room 20 minutes, judge what that means from 8.30pm to 8.00am. I had one patient dying and several others pretty near it. I have several very dangerously ill now – & one dying. I have 119 cases to look after in the acute lines. I caught a bit of a chill on Sunday & had to stay off duty again on Tuesday night, went on next night, but nearly right again now. There has been firing from the large guns several times tonight on a hill near here towards Wakkerstroom cannot see which, as it is too dark. Have not heard them for the last hour. You will see in Father's letter (hello! there are the guns again) about the Boer prisoners passing through in the train and the cattle being driven though. I lay in bed with my tent partially open and watched the noisy cattle coming across the Veldt. (Guns again). It makes one wonder what is going on. Colonel Daly's picnic on Tuesday next. We are going to Buffalo Valley (2½ miles away). We shall have to have an escort as it is out of our boundaries. It is in commemoration of our P.M.O. (Colonel Daly) receiving

a C.B. They do not interfere with duty at all & although it does not seem hardly the thing to be enjoying ourselves while fighting and sickness rages around. It is very necessary to have these little changes 'tis not as though we could call on friends or go shopping or to a theatre. There is absolutely nothing except what enjoyment we find for ourselves. Oh it is sad to see such fine men die & so many of them. We have a picnic given by my Medical Officer Mr. Crae & the Chaplain to Majuba some riding & some in the ambulance. We left horses and ambulance at the Blockhouse ¼ of the way up, & climbed to the top – a good stiff climb, but a magnificent view from the top. It is 7000ft high. We could see Laing's Nek, Buffalo Valley, Bothas' Pass, Spitz Kop where Plumer fought last week and many other places of note. We had the various positions explained to us & pictured it all with camps on the same night 21 yrs ago. A heavy mist came over just as we were going to take some snapshots, we were so disappointed, we took one of the place where Colley fell & and of the group of graves on the top of Majuba, but I think they will be a complete failure. We hope to go again & to have better success. We were so hungry & did ample justice to the tea ready for us when we returned. It looked very nice laid out on a cloth on the Veldt…
From this point the remainder of Katy's letter is missing.

This lady had entered a dangerous world. It was the time of the second Boer War: October 10th 1899 – May 31st 1902. All the place names she mentions had recently seen heavy fighting as the British pushed the Boers back across the 7000ft high Drakensberg Mountains which barred the way to the enemy's capital, Pretoria. I have no wish to add to the already extensive list of works dedicated to the study of this War, suffice it to say that "Enteric Fever" was responsible for more deaths in the British Army than the actions of the well equipped Boers. Exact figures are not easy to come across; during research for this book three different totals for casualty rates came to light. I have chosen the middle figures to illustrate the peril that these nurses had to face:

Killed In Action, or died of wounds –	7,582	
Died Of Disease –	13,259 –	(Enteric Fever accounted for 8000 deaths)
Wounded –	22,829	

These extremely brave women had to face this deadly killer on a daily basis; during the second year of the War, 1900, there are twenty-seven deaths recorded among the "Nursing Sisters". Rudyard Kipling was in South Africa as a journalist during the Boer War and his admiration of the work of the nurses is recorded in his poem 'Dirge of the Dead Sisters'. Prior to their landing in South Africa these women would have been fit, healthy and in their prime. As it was the virulent bacteria would overtake many of their number and they would die a lonely, lingering death thousands of miles from home. And the reason for all this grief? Polluted drinking water; apparently nothing can persuade the desperately thirsty from drinking water from any source they can find. Thirst is a desperate business; the unstoppable craving grows by the hour and in a land where supplies of water are uncertain, it is the natural instinct to avail oneself of whatever water is to hand.

There is a large and well-respected military hospital at Netley near Southampton. Working at Netley in the closing years of the nineteenth century was a Professor of pathology who had developed and proved safe, an anti typhoid vaccine; he submitted his report just as the war in South Africa broke out.

Katy left South Africa on November 8th 1902. She had come through a trial that many would not care to face. As her ship turned its bows northwards the girl from Sutton, who had already witnessed so much, would have turned her thoughts to home from which she had been absent for over two years.

Katy's return to Britain heralded yet another career change. We now find her working in London. This time private practice beckoned in the form of Dr Blacker who practised surgery, with consulting rooms in the famous Wimpole Street. She also provided care for the medical patients of Dr Parkinson who had rooms in Sloane Street. As well as her nursing work, Katy had become a qualified masseuse, a skill that was much in demand for patients recovering from surgery. At this period of her life we know that Katy was resident at 31, Eardley Crescent, Earlscourt, London SW15.

At a time when London was the largest and richest city in the world, Katy lived almost in the centre of its pulsating heart. People walked much more than we do today and for most ordinary folk their legs were the prime means of transport. Katy would have found a walk to Westminster (approximately 3 miles) followed by a stroll along the Thames Embankment, to go people-watching, as easy as falling off a log.

In Katy's now familiar style, her world did not stand still. The capital city itself couldn't hold her; she had seen broad horizons and a world most people only read or dreamed of. Her next foray saw her making an application for enrolment in Queen Alexandra's Imperial Military Nursing Service Reserve. Only those who came highly recommended were accepted. "Unsuitable appearance" as well as "unsatisfactory social status" meant automatic refusal. Katy submitted her application form on October 8th 1908. One pertinent question stands out from the others on the form: "What experience have you in the nursing of Enteric Fever?" Despite the appearance of a vaccine mentioned earlier, the Army Authorities still had a well-founded dread of the disease. Life has some strange twists and turns and in the main it is perhaps better that we cannot predict the future course of events. It is easy to read Katy's confident signature as a series of papers relating to her are retained at the Public Record Office at Kew. For Katy the die was now cast; by the act of attaching her name to the above-mentioned documents she and the Fates would collide, in the early hours of a winter morning in the Bristol Channel, in less than ten years time from the date of signing.

Katy's adventures next took her to Italy and to the capital city of that country, Rome. At the behest of the Italian Queen, Katy and five other Sisters had travelled to Rome to undertake the advanced training of local nurses, where she was lodged in the Royal Palace. Being of an enquiring nature we can imagine Katy making full use of her leisure time to observe the remains of Imperial Rome. Italy and the 'Eternal City' had been the favourite destination of the rich and famous for something like two-hundred years; here was Katy, the lass from Sutton, actually being paid to live there. It must have seemed as though a dream had come true. We know from family tradition and Katy's writings that she was a follower of the Anglican Religion. As the reader delves further into this work it will become obvious that nothing could hold her back; her outlook was more of how we see our times, not hers. The Vatican City and St. Peter's would have been high on her list to visit, despite their status as the headquarters of the Catholic Church on Earth. All that architecture, history and archaeology would have been an irresistible pull for Katy. Not for her the "twenty minutes here" on the coach 'tour' of the city that is only too familiar to our generation. To illustrate the last point the same did happen when two friends of mine visited Rome; the Coliseum – one of the most important buildings in the world dating back to AD 72 and the reign of the Emperor Vespasian, was only worth the legendary twenty minutes on the tour schedule. Katy lived in the world before mass tourism conquered the planet; everything that she wished to see she could do so at her leisure.

Her service to Italy was recognised by the award of a medal dated 1913 and so it is safe to assume that she returned home soon afterwards.

The planet we call home was not quiet; mighty and malignant forces were stalking the good Earth. In Europe a highly developed and sophisticated country,

Germany, headed by a cousin of our Royal Family, had come under the control of a group who continuously prepared for war with their neighbours. Diplomacy failed and the world began to slide into war. Germany unleashed her Armies westward through neutral Belgium as people everywhere looked on in horror. Britain's tiny Army, despatched to the aid of France and Belgium, collided with massively superior numbers of the enemy near the Belgian mining town of Mons. This was the end of the old way of life. The 'dogs of war' always bring with them to the table a diet of fear, uncertainty and despair. Great Auntie Katy, the Sister who had faced death when caring for typhoid victims from Exeter to the Transvaal, now faced journeys to the Middle East, the Mediterranean, the Dardanelles, France and South Wales all in the course of bringing relief to those who were suffering and as told in her own words in the diary she left behind.

Michael Harrison

4. KATY – WORLD WAR I

Katy volunteered for war service on August 17th 1914 and spent the first few months at Devonport Military Hospital. By June 4th 1915 she was at the No 15 General Hospital in the former Abbasieh School at Alexandria on which date she was transferred to the Ras-el-Din hospital there. She had her first ship, the Ionian, at Mudros which served the Gallipoli campaign after which she was appointed Matron of the New Khedivial Hotel at Alexandria, which had been a very grand hotel. In June 1916 she was appointed Matron of the Hospital Ship Dover Castle, a requisitioned steamship of the Union Castle Line for 607 patients. After nearly a year she was very fortunate to miss the torpedo

attack on her ship on May 26th 1917. She was invalided home from Inalla at Salonika because of inflamed haemorrhoids in order to have an operation. Later medical boards noted that the condition was as a result of nursing conditions at Salonika. She left on the Dover Castle for Malta on May 7th leaving behind two sisters and eight nurses because they transferred to the 29th General Hospital. Whilst on the island after May 18th she received a 'wire' which told her that her father Thomas had died on May 3rd and that she, as the unmarried daughter had inherited the house at Sutton Coldfield. She arrived in London on June 19th after using an

Katy – circa 1900.

13

overland route, probably via Marseille. On the 26th May the Dover Castle had been sunk by a torpedo attack north of Annaba, Algeria. Most of those on board were saved.

At home her operation was delayed until she could settle matters arising from the death of her father but it nevertheless took place on July 11th. She had already attended the Medical Board and over the following months she faced others on July 31 (Millbank, London) and August 30th and September 13th (both 1st Southern General Hospital, Birmingham). On the latter date she was pronounced fit for duty. Her address varied during this time but, most often, was her sister's home, Mrs Ellen Kirk, at The Grange, Shirley. She was in a hostel for nurses in London on October 31st when she learned that she was to be held in readiness for duty as Matron of the Hospital Ship Glenart Castle. On November 8th she received the nominal roll of nurses. When she compared it with the copy of the Senior Medical Officer she discovered that her salary was to be £75 per annum which was £10 less than previously. She wrote to the Matron in Chief to query the matter. On November 12th she left Euston for Liverpool and joined the ship the next day. Little is known about her service on the ship until the fatal attack at 3.47am on February 26th 1917. The ship sank in less than 10 minutes west of Lundy Island after the torpedo hit the engine room.

Gill Morgan

The War and Katy's Nephews – John Eric Beaufoy (known as Eric) and Clive Marston Beaufoy

Aida Beaufoy with Katy Tallis and John Eric.

John Eric in full Merchant Navy uniform, 1916.

John Eric with Katy in the garden, both invalided together! Recuperation together 1917, the last time Eric would see his Aunt.

John Eric Beaufoy

John Eric Beaufoy (b. 1898) the first child of John Beaufoy and Aida nee Tallis, of Stratford Road, Shirley, had a sister Katy Tallis born two years later, Katy after her aunt and Tallis after her mother. Eric was educated at Solihull School and at 13 left to train at the Merchant Naval Officer's Training School, HMS Worcester, based on the Thames, London, following certification joined the British India Shipping Company as a Midshipman. In January 1917 he and two fellow Midshipmen, having seen no action in the Great War, decided to jump ship and join in the fighting, they had to join the Australian army and hide the fact they were Merchant Navy Officers or would have been sent straight back to their ship. His two enthusiastic partners were to lose their lives in France, Eric kept Sinclair Bennitt May's (one of the partners) funeral memorial card all his life, (Eric's father was not best pleased having to pay £50 for breaking his indentures).

Eric was sent to France and was invalided out with trench fever firstly, and on a second occasion with influenza. This fortunately coincided with Great Aunt Katy's home leave for her surgery. Eric served until June 1919.

Katy Tallis (John Eric's sister and Katy Beaufoy's niece).

Clive Beaufoy

Clive, son of Katy's brother Samuel (who worked for a tea company in Ceylon), was sent back to England to be educated at Solihull School, at the age of 11 with his cousin John Eric (my father) living with his Aunt and Uncle, John and Aida Beaufoy at the Beeches Stratford Rd, Shirley, Solihull.

Clive kept a record of the daily mileage the ship covered on his return home from Columbo to London a journey of some three weeks, (copy of log in appendix).

Before enlisting into the army, Clive attended Solihull School, where he excelled at English, French and Science. He was also an excellent football player and was often mentioned in the 'Old Silhillians' magazine.

Eric and Clive – not all fun and games!

My father's anticipation of enjoying Clive's company wasn't entirely unalloyed, my father who had always received a beating when his sister Katy cried also received a beating when Clive was sick after a midnight feast of condensed milk (hidden on top of the wardrobe). To add insult to injury father had to learn to play the piano so Clive made sure he distracted him by kicking his football outside the window.

Father had been inspired by his Aunt Katy's tales of her adventures overseas in the Boer War and decided he would like to go to sea. As he was accepted into The Merchant Naval Officers Training School (HMS Worcester) he ruefully remarked that though he may get walloped with a rope end at least it would be for something he himself had done wrong!

Like his cousin Clive, he was good at sport was a rowing blue and also in the cricket first, the latter he enjoyed playing well into his 50's.

While with the British India Line he sailed extensively – his favourite country was New Zealand. He and my mother Elsie at last booked a two month holiday back to visit Australia and New Zealand in 1965, but he tragically died of a heart attack one week prior to embarkation.

Clive studied at Cambridge and was an original volunteer into the 2nd City Battalion Birmingham. He saw service in France before taking a commission and being posted to the 10th Royal Warwicks. The Battalion, which had twice been decimated, had reformed and was now back on the old battlefields, in the area of Aubers Ridge and Festubert. With only a few weeks more of warfare left the lads found themselves in the front line on Tuesday 24th September; leave was still being granted to a lucky few. An attack on the La Bassee Road had been planned for Wednesday 25th and this duly began at 8am led by 3rd Battalion

Worcs. Regiment. At 8.30am it was the turn of B Company 10th Warwicks to go over the top, and for a short time the attack wavered but was finally pressed home. The Germans were out for a fight and in no mood to give ground, pushing the Warwicks back a short distance. The War Diary tells us that the La Bassee Road position was not fully established until late and then only after 'much fighting'. Clive was killed during this attack; his death is recorded by name in the War Diary (appendices).

Clive is buried in Vielle Chapelle Military Cemetery on D170 road north of Bethune, France, Plot 8, Row C, Grave 9.

Erica Nadin-Snelling (née Beaufoy)
Gill Morgan

5. THE DIARY

(WITH PHOTOGRAPHIC INSERTS FOR THE PURPOSES OF THIS BOOK)

1915

10th MAY – Left Devonport Hos at 10.30am on May 10th 1915. Embarked on *'RMS Orsova'* on the same date as Commander Load, being the one who was Commander of the *'Orient'* when I returned from South Africa in Nov 1902. He informed me he had had a most anxious time since the war broke out. Once coming from Australia he had the *'Emden'* & 2 other enemy boats lying in wait for him & had also been chased. Always at night, had to go with all lights out, navigating lights as well. Had to stay in the Sound. While in the Sound we amused ourselves with watching all the others coming on board, as we were early arrivals. Mrs Parkinson accompanied us & stayed till 12 o/c, Matron & Mrs Hughes & some of the Sisters came down to the Dock gates but were not allowed on the Dock. They brought us books, sweets & other presents & sent them on board by one of the sergeants, with some letters also.

11th MAY – Still in The Sound, got to know a few of the other Sisters & were very interested in watching the Destroyers & Torpedo boats Submarines & other traffic (we lay off Torpoint). The men had all their life belts dealt out to them & hammocks & blankets, they slept with their heads on their belts

12th MAY – Still in The Sound & clear bright sunshine. Amused each other. Played my first rubber of quoits (first this time) 2 Officers & 2 Sisters, Captain & I won the rubber well ahead. Our decks were lined with men who had to put their hammocks straight on deck, side by side, then their blankets on top, their life belts under their heads & rifles, with extra ammunition, at their feet. Every other one had to stand with coats on, boots & stockings off, rifles in hand, keeping watch for so long, then they lay down & the others stood up. It was very amusing to hear their conversation. Suddenly one called out "U 13 Sir" at which there was a quiet laugh, as they were not supposed to make any noise. Then shortly after "I spy an aeroplane with light in starboard bow Sir" & so they beguiled the time, one growled & swore & so another said "be quiet darlint, don't swear" & he didn't. (Saw a cargo steamer.)

We were in The Sound till the night of the 12th, Wednesday, when we left shortly after midnight, being escorted by a Torpedo Destroyer till we had passed the breakwater. When the Destroyer came alongside, ordered all lights out & full steam ahead no matter what was in the way & full steam ahead we went. As the Captain said "we should have smashed anything in the way".

Next morning we were awakened by a flash of light in the cabin, in spite of the venetian blinds, which we were told was the searchlight from the Destroyer accompanying, but the Captain says "No, it may have been when they were changing the dynamo as the Destroyer left us at the breakwater & went back to fetch the other 2 troop ships & the one for horses & fodder, of which we have not had any news since we left, though they were ready before we left".

Sister Brown is sharing the cabin with me, S.N.Bodey & S.N.F.R.Smith (the other Devonportonions) in a cabin opposite.

13th MAY – In the Bay of Biscay 'O'- she behaved in a fairly rough manner – not so bad as in December 1900 or 1901, but I felt pretty seedy. Did some writing, reading, walking, eating & drinking only. Saw another ship but too far off to see what.

Poor Bodey gave up on Thursday morning till Friday tea, since which she has been well. S.Brown & myself had to stay from dinner on Thursday evening.

14th MAY– Rather shaky on the morning of Friday the 14th.

Some thunder & lightening. Felt better – played quoits, 2 games 1-1, did not finish the rubber, felt a bit too seedy. Vaccinated in the afternoon. Very well after & enjoyed dinner. Much warmer.

15th MAY– Not quite so warm & duller, but towards evening became brighter & the sea more blue.

16th MAY – Arrived at Gibraltar 6.30am, had my bath & dressed at once & went on deck. An old Italian Torpedo Destroyer hovered round. We went close to the harbour but not inside till about 2.30pm. We had to wait for a Cruiser to come out, then we took her place. When we were close in, the crane took off a big gun, she looked a beauty. The Spanish men in the stores brought such quantities of cigarettes & matches, also cigars & one very large one for the Officers. The men had 100's of small pkts. I should think from one & another & one man who had bought a lot himself for them, stopped every man & boy & asked of all. It was fun to see them empty their pockets. After one had given his cigarettes & the gentleman had left him, he suddenly put his hand in his coat & pulled out a good sized tin of baccy & flung it to the men. Several made a grab & the tin went in the sea. They did clap the man. A boy stood near with a clean basket going marketing, they borrowed his basket, tied a piece of string to the handle & fished up the tin safe & sound.

When we went away there was such barracking & cheering & shouts of "He is a jolly good fellow".

We had early service on Ascension Day to which I went, several had to come out without taking part, but were enabled to do so this morning. We had services fore & aft, some Officers & Sisters going to each. A few very appropriate words from the Parson. We have 4 Chaplains on board, 2 going to Egypt & 2 to Malta. The Territorial Sisters are going to Malta. I should think they would want to commandeer us, according to the figures in the wireless news of 40,000 wounded taken there from the Dardanelles. In the afternoon, just before going right into harbour, we saw a welcome sight, 'The Hiberinia', our 2nd troop ship, come in. There was a welcome on both sides. She was one that listed so much to l'arboard [*starboard] when in D'port [*Devonport]. We had wondered so much where she was. She had run across our bows dragging her anchor in Plymouth, however she was better balanced in Gibraltar & left soon after our 3rd troop ship passed, the latter not coming into harbour. We left about 5 o/c & passed the other boats about 7pm. It was a lovely evening, the lights from the after glow splendid. We had the armed guard all round again, as from then are to have them night & day for the rest of the voyage. We expect to be at Malta on Wednesday & may have to stop 2 days.

17th MAY – Not so warm as yesterday evening but warm & bright, sea a lovely blue. Passing the African coast, which appears as a cloud. 3.50pm off coast of Algiers. 1st fire drill at 4.45pm. We were watching a game of quoits when suddenly the fire alarm bell went & up came stokers, firemen, sailors, cabin boys, waiters, Officers & men to take their places. The Sisters having to make a hasty & ignominious retreat to the Drawing room where some of us put our heads out of the window to watch proceedings – then the siren went off – two awful shrieks – these being a signal for the boats to be launched. After dinner we had a very good concert on deck. All lights had to be out by 11 o/c.

Had some good strawberries from Gibraltar.

18th MAY – A lovely day, arms feeling painful, 4th day of vaccination. We are busy writing for the mail for Malta. Boxing matches on board, not anything of importance happened.

19th MAY– We arrived at Malta, in the harbour about 8.40 o/c but didn't go into the harbour till 9.30am or thereabouts. The Admiralty were cross because the Captain did not go quickly in & asked "what he was messing about for". I suppose that was because we were all packed expecting to disembark, but received no orders & so remained as before. The guards were doubled & officers, they had seen 3 German submarines in the Mediterranean & so they were anxious. We put off all the Terriers & 12 Reserve Sisters at Malta, about 50 in all. 202 R.A.M.C. men & non C.O's & about 20 Officers of R.A.M.C & Regts. The troops & most of the Officers are still on board. Malta is as if built in 3 distinct parts & is very much larger than I thought. It is well fortified, looks as if there were huge walls nearly all round the island. The cliffs seem to be of a yellow sand. There were only French boats in the harbour (I mean Men of War). One French cruiser on our left decorated her boat very gaily with flags in our honour. There was a French submarine went out & passed us close, almost brushing us, such a curious one in shape & the whole surface flat. I think I managed to snap her alright, but my camera (the finder) wants cleaning, but I must use the films first now. We are told not to be alarmed if we see a submarine as the French one is out. Two cruisers (French) went out before us but now we cannot see them. We left about 2.30pm we were not allowed to land. As we entered, the naval hospital, a fine building built in pavilions with balconies, stood on our left.

The Royal Naval Hospital, Valetta – 2003.

The patients were out on the balconies in their beds & we could see Drs, Sisters & Orderlies in white, attending them. It has been quite chilly & we were pleased to change our cotton dresses for woollen ones. We had put on cotton knowing it would be hot if we landed. There was the usual numbers of boats with things for sale & divers, diving for money. At 4pm it became rather warmer & bright & the sea was again the true Mediterranean blue.

Miss Hoadley, Matron of Q.A.I.M.N.S.R. Malta.

20th MAY – We passed the two troop ships last evening about 8pm & did not see them after. Had a concert last evening – fairly good. Tonight had a smoking concert on well deck (Tommy's) & very well they did.

21st MAY– Arrived at Alexandria, waited outside for tug for some time, then went inside & anchored there for the night about 6pm. There seemed to be hundreds of ships in the harbour. Very large number of troop ships & ones to go to the Dardanelles in the morning. There are some German ships, prizes, now used as troop ships. A large French cruiser with 2 groups of 3 large funnels & 1 in the middle (7 in all) an old pattern they say, she steamed out at sunset.

22nd MAY – Saturday, still waiting orders 11 o/c. News came about 12 o/c that our hospital had not arrived (by that, I understand equipment.) So we are to split up till it arrives, & then unite again. I believe we are going with Matron to No 15 General Hospital.

23rd MAY – 10.30pm – We disembarked at about 11.30am & went ashore on a baggage barge, a huge flat thing. Luggage on 1 barge & Officers & men were with us on the other. It took about ½ hour to get to shore & there we stood in the sun. On shore we sought a little shade, there were some stores with an iron rail running round a little distance away from the walls for tethering horses & some had been there recently. There were 8 chaplains & very jolly men, just the sort for our men, for they were earnest men as well. These all joined us on the rail, there we sat till the baggage had been put on shore. Then the sorting commenced & each pointed out their own (all marked) & had it placed together. Then the cabs [Karrozzin]

Karrozzin.

23

similar to the Italian Carrotza drove up & we got in, 4 in each. We were driven
through a sort of Whitechapel at first – houses very like the Italian. After about a
¼ hour we got to the cleaner streets & better shops & at last to the Hospital high
upon the hill (a school with tents round). It contains 1,800 beds. They have been
very busy, when started it was not intended for Sisters, but they have had
thousands of cases here & No 17, so they commandeered the Colonial & Civil
nurses who were private nursing, then some Territorials from Malta went, & from
England. They are very busy now so we are helping till ours is ready. I go on
tomorrow morning with 8 more & 9 go on in the afternoon. We were intended for
Rabbit Island, I hope we shall go. When we arrived at Hospital after waiting some
time, we were sent off in motor ambulances to the Hotel Regina to lunch. They are
to board us & as they have not rooms, they got some at the Hotel Grand Suisse
where S.Brown & I share a room. We then had to go back & see Matron. After
which we had tea, unpacked a few necessary articles in our room (S.Brown & I)
got ready for dinner, Matron giving me a list of names, half for the morning duty
& half for aft. I was on in the morning. We slept the night at Hotel Grand Suisse,
3 minutes away from the Regina Palace Hotel, where we boarded or messed. Mr
Asquith's youngest son, who had been injured in the knee, was there on crutches.
Another of his sons had been there wounded. General (King?) was living there,
he was the Commanding Officer of the District.

24th MAY – Went to breakfast 7 o/c the ambulance came for the Sisters, but
could not take all, 4 were left after the second call, so an automobile being near,
the chauffeur offered to drive us over. He took us all through the main streets to
see the decorations for the Sultan's procession the morning previous (while we
were on the boat) but we saw him the same evening out driving with an outrider
& one on either side on motorcycles (he was in a motor). We had to wait some
little time after we arrived at the Hospital to see the Matron (Miss Grierson)
who eventually told us where to go. I had a ward of about 50 beds, such bad, bad
wounds frightful head ones, legs & feet blown off, & arm wounds of all sorts.
The Sister, having 108 could not go into this ward which was left to the orderly.
The Doctor & he doing the dressings, some beds have not been made for 3 days
& lockers & other things in a very dirty & untidy state which was not the fault of
the workers, sheets were very dirty & counterpanes. I did some of the dressings
& made up some of the beds with clean linen, leaving quite half the beds clean &
patients comfortable & had all the lockers turned out & scrubbed. When I went
to tea I was informed I must pack & be off to Ras-el-Tin by 6 o/c. The transport
did not come, so telephoned & arranged for it to come at 8.30pm, after we had

finished dinner, so we arrived about 9.30pm. It is the quaintest place, entering through archways (2) we arrived in a square in the centre, lovely gardens laid out with geraniums, flowers similar to dwarf marigolds, cynthie & many others, bouganvilla, orianthus (big red flowers). On one side are Sisters quarters 2 med. Officers & administration offices. Round the other two sides were wards & between the archways a way leading to Officers & other wards & stores to right & left of the archways. One storey high only (all the buildings). The open way from the square leads out to the lighthouse a few yards away, our hospital etc being built on the point. The convalescent pts being in tents outside our arches, between us & the German prisoners & on beyond the Sultan's Palace (10 minutes walk away) & then barracks. At the back of our cottages are small but bright gardens with verandas, hung with various creepers with bright flowers. We have most of our meals out of doors under cover of veranda, at the bottom of the little garden. Not 12 yards away is the sea (the side of the harbour where our wounded are brought to our pier). On the other side is the open sea coming close up, all the men who are able, can have their sea bath providing they are properly equipped. Miss Bond (the Matron) who was my Super at Charleston S.A. in 1902, was pleased to see me. I was asked "would I have Officers or men's ward", preferred the latter & have 3 & 4 Surgical. Have some very bad cases, two shot through the lungs, pouring out pus. One amputation who had had his foot blown off & part of his leg, with 3 other bad wounds in various parts of his body (shrapnel). 2 other amputations, 2 fractured thighs, 1 cerebro hernia (paralysis) right of arm & leg, shoulders, arms, some of the latter by bayonet, others shoulders, chest, legs & feet.

25th MAY – Went on duty to the above ward where a little Red Cross nurse was in charge & did very well considering, was off duty in the evening. Put up my camp bed as I had to go into room with Bodey. There are 4 rooms, ours a passage room & all rooms go out from one to the other. Very hot wind off land, sand storm wind from the desert.

26th MAY – On duty in 3 & 4, the nurse Miss Jentell (lives in Egypt) having gone to another ward. Off in the afternoon for an hour, had a bath & cleaned my shoes & it was tea time, after which I went on duty till 7.20 one of the lung cases (Lear) had a tube put in the wound some 6 in long & out poured the vilest pus, 4 good sized kidney trays full. Arranged tube & bottle similar to op. for bile – had 2 1lb bottles full in 26 hrs. Patient much relieved in breathing, as the pressure was very great on the only useful lung. Temp. normal, previously 102 or 103°.

27th MAY – Above patient much better, breathing quieter & slower. Off duty in the evening. Went with Sr Smith to Alexandria to see Sr Brown at the Regina Palace Hotel, where we had been staying. Had a chat & heard of 5 of ours (intended for WXIX)[No 19 Hosp] having been sent to Cairo. We went to buy some muslin & apples & then returned by cab (5d for the two) through the quaintest parts of the city, all gaily decorated with arches & flags. We passed great numbers of cafes with men sitting outside or in, smoking their opium pipes (this was very sad as some looked so young). The houses, many in this part were overhanging, some had pretty balconies or windows, others dark looking places, one could easily imagine inside to be a place of darkest crimes. The women of the higher classes dress as Europeans but the others wear black cloaks & black or white cloths covering their mouths & faces, all but their eyes, & hanging down low. They are kept away from mouths by what look like bamboo tubes, propped between their eyes & somewhere below their noses. Some wear white veils (cooler) most of the men wear fez of red with a black tassel, as does the Sultan himself.

28th MAY – I heard today of the plot of the natives in January. It was discovered 2 days before it was to be carried into operation. A little Syrian maid, who was much implicated, got frightened & confessed. The plan was to destroy every white man & woman, English, French & Italian. That is why the soldiers (Australian) were landed here instead of going straight to the Dardanelles. They now keep a good number here. In country places just outside Alex. they look very menacing if our men go by.

27th JUNE – Nothing of importance has happened since I last wrote. On this day paid my 1st visit to a private house, Mr Dartons' house, 14, Marina, Alex. (c/o John Ross & Co, of whose business he is a manager). Joe is the friend of Dickie's with whom she stayed when on a visit here. It is a fine old place, over a century old, some of its ceilings are very fine specimens of Egyptian gilding & painting at that period. I met there Dickie's chum who was at the Sudan with her. Mrs Stephenson & her husband, very pleasant people, also Capt. who was Commander of a troop ship & was returning to the Dardanelles that night with troops. He had had a narrow escape the week before. A German submarine suddenly appeared too close to him to alter his course or to move. Immediately she fired a torpedo & he waited, expecting a big shot. When looking over the other side, he saw the torpedo disappearing, having gone under without touching. The submarine also had disappeared. There were known to be two about between Alex. & the Dardenelles.

1st JULY – We went to the Stephensons at Mustafa Pasha. Joey met us at Ramleh & she, Bodey & I thoroughly enjoyed our train ride to Mustafa, past the troops, transport & barracks which were along the road between the left side & the sea. The horses seemed in fine condition. Many had been taken to the Dardanelles, but could not be landed & were brought back. We met the Stephensons & went down to the beach at Stanley Bay. The black flag was out, showing there was a rough & dangerous sea on for bathing, but many men were enjoying it but did go far out. The waves were fine as they rolled in & dashed among the rocks, or on the beach. The cliffs were fairly high, reminding me a little of Babbacombe Bay. Along the bottom were numerous bathing sheds, built smartly & used as boathouses where they came for tea as well as bathing. At our end were those of the soldiers & the other, private ones. Mr Asquith's son & daughter used one next but one to the Stephensons. Sir Henry & Lady MacMakon came down. Many convalescent Officers & men were there, French, Australian & New Zealand as well as ours.

9th JULY – The 2nd attack on the Sultan since the end of May – a bomb was thrown at his car while driving from the Yacht Club, Ras-el-Tin to the palace. Fortunately although it hit the car it did not burst.

14th JULY – Left Alexandria on the 'Galeka' at 10am – Union Castle Line. We did not leave Ras-el-Tin till 11pm (S.Chapman & I) Matron accompanied us to the gates. We had to feel our way to the Yacht Club, only to find all in darkness & the door shut. We felt our way carefully to the side, saw a little light & 2 Arab men whom we could not make understand we were going to embark from their pier. They would insist on showing us the front door, thinking we had lost our way. We saw our launch (belonging to the coastguards) approaching, pointed to it & ran off down the pier. We arrived on board about 12 midnight – had rather a pokey cabin & slept very little.

15th JULY – Were inoculated against cholera. The Hosp. ship 'Arturias' passed with 1,500 on board.

16th JULY – Had a splendid night, we came in sight of the first land about 10.30am. Passed Rhodes & 2pm passed a large group of islands. Went round to see the wards on the boat & to make notes for a future occasion.

17th JULY – Lemnos 1st seen about 10am as a cloud. At the same time we saw a transport in distress on our left. A '42' (said to have been a prize during the early part of the year & to have been very useful to us since). Her stern was nearly touching the water & her bow nearly out of water. Another boat stood by her all the way till she arrived safely in harbour, which at times looked as if it could not possibly do. As we neared her we could see that she had been in collision & was badly damaged on right side of stern, opposite the stern mast above the water line. We arrived just inside the harbour at 1pm & at 1.30 moved into the inner part. We found about 16 French war ships & 1 Russian cruiser 'Smoke' – the one badly damaged at Port Arthur by the Japs, but she has done good work here. She has 5 funnels (at one end only). There was the Naval Hosp. ship plying to & from Malta & 3 others, the 'Somali' (naval), 'Reiva' & 'Auralia' (Sudan). We hear we are the 3rd ship to go to Cape Helos but what happens to us we know not (Dr's, Sisters & Ord. 50). The Captain & Colonel Sir Mayo Robson (an eminent surgeon) went to see if there were any orders but No, there were not. Lemnos is a fine island, hilly with a few groups of trees & bright green patches of vegetation in (probable crops) here & there, a small village at the extreme end of the bay, & on the right, a little town with apparently a fine Greek church on the hill. Our camp is near this, & then there are the Australians & 2 French camps, we could see them drilling & some exercising their horses in the water & on land.

18th JULY – Had service on board at 10am. At the service recognised Dr. Ravenhill who had a long chat with me afterwards. I learnt he had been 5 months in Serbia & afterwards to Malta & now he had come to inoculate for cholera, on the peninsula (Gallipoli). He had joined in Sept. & was for a while in camp in England. The 'Auralia' Hosp. ship & the 'Reiva' gone to Dardanelles. 2.30 Dr Ravenhill gone to Dardanelles with 4 others to inoculate against cholera. The 'Mauritania' & 'Aquitania' still in. 1st saw them as we entered harbour.

20th JULY – The 'Neuralia' Hosp. ship came in filled with wounded.

21st JULY – The 'Sudan' left for Malta with wounded on board.

22nd JULY – 11.30 the troop ship 'Knight Errant' came into harbour filled with troops. At 2 o/c went for a sail & landed at Talikna, a village on Lemnos Island. It was harvest & they were gathering the harvest in. They had tied the beans & what looked like the gray pea

The wheat is not so white as ours. *in a small pod so ( )* They had some broad beans dried

also. All these things they tie in bundles like wheat, they then sit down like the

Italians & beat them with a stick. They then collect the beans & put them in a sieve which is fastened to a stick in the ground, about 4 foot high. The chaff for the cattle seems mostly straw, they place it in a circle then 2 oxen are yoked & they pull what seems to be a sort of wooden sledge with knives under it, on which stands a girl of about 14 or a woman. These go constantly round & round, thus breaking the brittle straw. Then they fastened several donkeys together & they are made to run round quickly, thus breaking it quite fine. Vegetable marrows were quite good, grapes were not well looked after, they were small green ones. There were mellons, but small ones. There were, in some bits of gardens, scented geraniums. Growing wild were 2 different kinds of yellow thistles, some flowering rushes (blue), leaves like mimosa, thorns for sharpness, also several other very pretty ones. We went into the old church (Greek) which was very clean, but to me nothing very extraordinary. Some of the older paintings on wood were good but there was not anyone who could tell us if they were valuable or not (I think not). They had a great fancy for lace curtains which were hung all round & everywhere they could get. We saw the women spinning on little hand distaffs. We went into one of their houses, one in which the daughter had been to America for 4 years & had been back 2 years, for her Mothers sake. I do not think she would stop after her Mother no longer needed her. We went up the wooden stairs to her rooms above, all very clean & draped with white muslin curtains with crochet work. The girl had done her best & all was in order & showed good taste, but the arrangements were quaint, the bed was stripped & put up folded against the wall & everything tidy. The walls were rough, the outside of stone & the inside walls of rushes & mud. The inside of the upper rooms were whitewashed but downstairs rough & the floors just rough mud. The men wore very baggy seated trousers & hats (various), the women peculiar stockings & slippers without heels. On their heads h'dkfs [*handkerchiefs] of lawn & neat trimming, such as narrow lace or beads. In some of the villages they weave cloth, but not in this. We wended our way back to the boat & were carried by the sailors through the water to our boat (2 waded). When our boat arrived we found 110 wounded or sick men had arrived & the ship's staff of Sisters busy. We set to work to help. We expect to be transferred shortly to another boat as this will go out to Alex when full. They are expecting a Turkish attack & they say they will drive us all into the sea. We shall see. Our sick men, who in addition to the above, came in after dinner, look so tired & worn, poor men, the strain has told on them fearfully. The 'Somali' Hos. Ship went.

23rd JULY – Told to pack up, but a false alarm. Very stiff after yesterday. Inoculated for cholera the 2nd time. Many more wounded arrived, 13 stretcher

& many others, after tea. After dinner many stretcher cases, the minor cases were sent to the island. The *'Gloucester Castle'* Hosp. ship came in. She is of this line, fitted up in England in the latest style, an electric bell over each bed & hot & cold water in each ward. In the Officers – walls are painted a delicate colour, over each swing cot is a bell, pulley & electric fan. The *'Grantulli Castle'* Hosp. ship came in from Cape Helas with wounded on board.

24th JULY – Left the *'Galeka'* & went on board the Allam line *'Ionian'* to await the transports, the Captn & Officers welcoming us most heartily. After dinner the *'Rewa'* Hosp. ship came in loaded with patients, she had filled up at Cape Helas & came to report. There is another Hosp. ship in. The *'Galeka'* left at 6 o/c this morning. Some wounded were put on the *'Gloucester Castle'* last evening & this morning on the new arrival.

25th JULY – Sunday – heard firing several times in the afternoon (& in the early morning at 3am there was some). Then again about 6.30pm we heard & saw a huge cloud of dust go upward from a little bit of an island in the harbour, close to one of the ships. This morning they inflated a balloon on the ship purposely altered for them. After 2 or 3 hrs they let the air out, our Officers thought they were sending it to reconnoitre to see why the firing was, but that the wind was too strong. It has been very hot today, I think it must have been another Khamsine. There has been much movement among the troops. It seemed to me they are transferring them to two lower built boats, but larger ones. I saw Capt'n who was on the *'Orsova'* with us. He tells me all the Worcester Officers are believed to be killed, missing or wounded & ¾ of the Officers from the *'Orsova'* killed or wounded. The perspiration is streaming down me while I write. It is 11.25pm. I have an electric fan in my cabin (the only Sister here with one, as I am Senior & in charge).

27th JULY – Went for a picnic on shore at the back of the island in outer harbour. Officers from *'H.M.S. Doris'* Mr Allen, Mr Goodyear, Mr Wace, Dr. Melrose, Mr Twinning. Had a good time & a good sail back. We passed the Isle of Man paddle steamer *'Queen Vic'* & saw the vessel which we had passed on our way to Alexandria, after she had been run into by a French Man of War. The bows of the French ship were badly damaged. There are about 30 war ships in.

28th JULY – Went for a picnic. Dr Thomas P.M.O. taking the place of Melrose. Went to the same place, we made the tea while the men went further on for a bathe. Three of our submarines in.

29th JULY – Went for a sail round the harbour leaving Dr Tatum on the 'Minnetonga', called at the 'Aregan' then sailed round, getting a good view of the Australian camp & hospital, men, tents & sand being hardly distinguished at a distance. An airship flew over very early, 3am, dropped 2 bombs outside the harbour & ———

30th JULY– Went for a sail to the 'Minnetonga', Dr Tatum coming down again to ask us to come on board. So we (three Sisters) went up & were introduced to Col. Cochrane, who is in charge of all the ammunition for this part of the war centre. I found I have met him several times before, at Volkstrust & Charlestown. There was such an enormous stock of ammunition on board, shells 60lbs & 70 lbs each, 14 & 16 in & boxes of bullets of every kind. He showed us some hand bombs, Turkish, they were smooth & round like an orange, with an opening on one end with a small projecting piece of iron from the   *Lid &c*
 At the extreme end of the curved piece was the fuse or brimstone like cap. From the inside of the lid the detonator went down into the powder, the inside of the shell was made in small squares over the surface. The fuse was ignited by rubbing on emery paper fastened on to the tunic. They roll them on the ground & sometimes our men catch them & send them back, but unless very quick they explode in their hands. They are beautifully made. Ours are mostly of milk (condensed) tins etc. I saw some of their 12 in (Turks) shells, empty, which had not burst, the driving band like mine, some were filled with sand. At 9.30pm we noticed peculiar flashes in the sky. On going up to the Bridge deck we could see better, & the Commander & Officers & 3 visitors (2 Naval Lts.) went up with us. It was guns, they kept it up incessantly till about 1.30am, but I did not see after. We all wondered, but of course could not find out & doubtless you will know before we do. We could not make out if it was on sea or land but it moved so much in the time, it seemed to me to be on sea (always in the same direction). They say it could be 30 – 40 miles distant. The fleet surgeon had been on board in the afternoon to see the ship, if fitted for a Hosp. ship. Several war ships had gone out in the early morning. These things we cannot put in our letters.

31st JULY – On board this morning there does not seem a breath of wind. The sea is like a mill pool & the haze over the hills gives promise of great heat. A submarine has just gone out. She is longer than our earlier ones, have not seen the latest, with masts on. The 'Mauritania' & 'Aquitania' have been gone some days. The 'Caledonia' & many fine vessels are still in. There are now 11 Divisions (about 220,000 men) here, ready for the Asiatic movement. Capt. Caine came on board from the 'Devanha' P.& O. & took 3 of us back to lunch, so I gave Sister Brown a surprise. She, the Hosp. ship is arranged very nicely & in very good order. At 4pm we went in the 'Cornwallis' pinnace, to a concert on board got up by the crew & enjoyed it very much, returning at 7.15pm for dinner. At 10pm there was a heavy gun fire again, after which a little wind came, but it had been a fearfully hot day, the hottest here since we arrived in the bay. Capt'n Davidson is in command of 'H.M.S. Cornwallis'. The 'Delta' arrived.

1st AUGUST – We had a visitor Lt. Seaton (engineer) who said it was gun fire at the Dardanelles as they had communication from there about it, but what result, he of course could not say. When on board the 'Cornwallis' I was told by an Officer that there were 50 new Lighters in England, of the kind to land the troops under cover, the landing stage being pulled out by machinery from underneath the deck, where the troops are hidden. These are said to be for landing troops on the Dutch shores within 2 weeks time. The Dutch – not to declare war against our enemy till our troops are actually landed.

2nd AUGUST – The 'Devanha' was loaded yesterday. Today the 'Galeka' came in & this afternoon recd. her 1st lot of patients. The 'Salicia' came in. 6 med Officers & 30 Orderlies arrived from the 'Delta'. Gen. Sir Porter came on to inspect the boat. The boat recd a very satisfactory report. A hydroplane boat came in this morning & went out this evening. We saw one of the planes, but not in use.

3rd AUGUST – Recd word that we were to be an ambulance carrier & I was to be in charge. Mattresses, pillows are to be sent on board before 12 o/c (one pt. died at 6am). At 7pm wounded (143) arrived but not any mattresses, we borrowed all we could from the ship till ours arrived. Most of the cases were enteric, dysentery & diarrhoea & a few surgical.

4th AUGUST – 67 more cases arrived of the same kind. Capt. Bennett arrived as O/C.

5th AUGUST – 268 more cases in the morning & 233 at 6.30pm. Mt Anderson as 2nd in command.

8th AUGUST – Too busy a time to write (arrived outside harbour 8pm).

9th AUGUST – Went into docks at Alex. & disembarked the men (one – *Goodfellow – died at 8.30am). All off by 1pm. Went to Ras-el-Tin after 3pm (saw Lady Carnaevon in the morning & Mrs Rufers, who obtained clothing for me, shirts, socks etc.). I had a hearty welcome at Ras-el-Tin among my friends, Bodey ret'd with me for dinner, going back with S.Keen, who had to leave me. S.Cooper taking her place (rec'd over 20 letters).

10th AUGUST – Went ashore to see about Red X things & about pay. Left Alex. again at 2 o/c.

11th AUGUST – Several Hosp. ships passed in the night, so it looks as if we were going to be busy.

12th AUGUST – Arrived Windros Bay at about 8pm.

*N.B. Pte Albert Henry Goodfellow, No:9527 5th Batt. Wiltshire Regiment
Born – Chilmark, Wiltshire, Enlisted – Salisbury, Resided – Chilmark
Buried – Alexandria (Chatby) Cemetery

13th AUGUST – We were told we must go on the same evening, but about 8 or 8.30 the 'Royal Edward', who took our berth in Alex. to embark troops & follow us up, was torpedoed by submarine just outside the harbour, 1,100 troops & about 400 crew, a few hundred only, saved. A destroyer rushed out to rescue them, our having the distress S.O.S signals. There have been about 10,000 casualties this last week, one boat took 1,100, another 1,800. The 'H.M.S. Doris' hit pretty badly, lost 2 guns, not sure about loss of life, hope none of our friends are lost – nothing much gained as yet at the Dardanelles – a fresh landing certainly, but naught else. It is fearful. The E. Lancs & Manchesters got between 2 hills & were completely wiped out. Two new Sisters came from the 'Simla' at 11.30pm, B.Henderson S.N. & S.A.O'Riordan S.N.

14th AUGUST – Lt. Reid put on shore (diarrhoea) & Lt. King put in his place. Orders to go to outer harbour for wounded. Mr Allan came on board from 'H.M.S. Doris' & said that she had not been hit at all & not lost men or guns.

15th AUGUST – 'Aquitainia' went out with (I hear) 3,000 wounded on board. We have sent 20,000 wounded away from Dardanelles in a week. Yesterday – lost again the hill we had gained. More troops gone up in a destroyer. The

'*Formosa*' came alongside & we took 526 patients (150 cot cases) off. Many of the cases very bad indeed. Some had been 3 & 4 days on board. 26 cases were Officers. Went to bed 2am.

16th AUGUST – Monday – Arose at 6.30am, busy till 12 midnight.

18th AUGUST – Left Mudros.

21st AUGUST – Arrived at Malta 6am spent the night at St Paul's Bay.

22nd AUGUST – Retd to another harbour at Malta (Valetta) disembarked the walking cases in the morning, the cot cases in the afternoon & evening. Just after 7.20pm the word came down – 17 cot cases had been returned – the '*Gondola*' (H.S.) had given the wrong number of beds & so the poor fellows had to return to us & get that extra move with another extra one next morning. Our walking cases went on shore, the cot cases to the '*Gondrea*'.

23rd AUGUST – We finished the disembarking of our 750 patients, the remainder going on board the '*Andania*', who like the '*Gondola*' was bound for England, as we were when we left Mudros Bay, but were informed we must

Church of St. John, Valetta.

disembark our pts. & return to Mudros. We lost 8 pts. on our way, 4 surgical & 4 med. We went on shore in the afternoon, saw the Church of St John with some very fine copies of originals & some fine originals (Italian), also the mosaic was fine.

We did some shopping & I went to Red X stores. Got a promise of many things to be down at the quay by 10am (but the boat leaving at 6am – did not get them). After dinner we retd to shore & went to visit some of the Sisters at the married qrtrs. We learned that it was true that the 'Royal Edward' was lost a few hours (12) after we had passed over the spot & 1,100 were lost. The 'Scotian' also was reported sunk, hope it is not true, Drs & Sisters were aboard. Our boat moved to Grand Harbour.

We had heavy showers about 4am & had to lift the stretcher cases from under the awning into the wards. Showery during the day, which made it much more pleasant for us, cooler, to get about Malta.

24th AUGUST – Left about 7.45am with instructions to take another course as 3 submarines were about the eastern part of Mediterranean & the Aegean Sea.

25th AUGUST – Much warmer.

26th AUGUST – Dreadfully hot night, warm winds (scirocco). Heavy thunder storms.

27th AUGUST – Arrived near Lemnos, but too late to enter harbour so cruised about till early next day.

28th AUGUST – Went into harbour about 6 o/c in the morning, found 'Dwana', 'H.S. Gloucester Castle' & 3 other H. ships & many troop ships.

29th AUGUST – 'Valdivia' H.S. came alongside & we took 506 patients from her, mostly enteritis & dysentery, a few wounded & some enterics. We left the harbour same evening for Malta. Had a chat with some of the Officers who say very little is being done, a new landing was accomplished & that was practically all. A big movement is expected shortly. Our men have mostly been out for 17 weeks & look ill & fagged out.

We left at 5.30pm for Malta, having 514 pts on board only & one Orderly, Beavan, very ill with dysentery. Had a good passage & less work as most of the patients were much better than the previous ones.

1st SEPTEMBER – We arrived at Malta, disembarked the pts on shore & went on shore in the evening. We disembarked in the quarantine harbour after (next morning) 5.30 going into Grand Harbour. Very hot day – scirocco.

2nd SEPTEMBER – Went to see Miss Hoadley, the Principal Matron of Malta, whom I had not seen since I was in S.A. at Charlestown. She looked well & was very pleasant. Sister Cooper & I afterwards did some shopping, went on shore to lunch, retd after seeing everything was going on all right & did some more shopping, Mr King & Mr Allan accompanying us. We retd at 4.30 & left Malta about 6pm. 12 new Officers came on board as passengers. It had been very hot but we had our stores all right from the ordnance & Red Cross. Mr Nobb new M.O. on board.

3rd SEPTEMBER – Felt very poorly, sick & pains all over me, more neuralgic in character. Got up, went to see the wards were being put into order, sat on deck a while, then went to bed till next morning. Very hot day (still scirocco).

4th SEPTEMBER – Feeling better, but about 10.30 my legs commenced paining again & my back, however, went round the wards, found them very well done & all the equipment being cleaned. Lay down in a hammock on bridge deck from 1.45 till 8pm, felt better. Lt Duget R.N.Res. gave a lecture previous night on the attack on Zeebrugge (very good I heard) I could not go, being in bed.

5th SEPTEMBER – Sunday – Early services this morning. We have R.N.Chaplain C of E & one R.C. on board. They had been home with the patients, over 2,000 on the 'Aquitania' & were returning for duty with the fleet here, were put on shore at Malta till we came, when they came on board our boat. Most of the passengers are naval men, there is a Staff Major Collins & several lieuts, military.
   Had 2 very good services on board.

6th SEPTEMBER – Arrived in Alex. outer harbour. We were told we should be in for 2 hrs so I obtained permission to go in a boat to Ras-el-Tin & Sr Cooper to go to 21 G.H. for the letters. When we retd there was no order.

7th SEPTEMBER – We were told to go to 18 wharf & there, were told that the 'Ionian' must carry troops.

8th SEPTEMBER – We were informed that we must transfer to the 'Gloucester Castle' Hosp. ship, but not till 5 o/c, so Sr Cooper, with Lt Ganad & Lt Brown went for a drive, first calling on Miss Oram. Then we drove to Nouzah Gdns, where we had lunch consisting of cakes, biscuits, apples & Schweppes ginger beers. We thoroughly enjoyed our first visit to the gdns. Afterwards we drove along the Mahmondick Canal, where, on either side were sugar plantations (canes), cotton, mealies, any amount of dates nearly ripe. The native huts & houses were very quaint & dirty, as was the muddy water. We came out on the far side of Mustafa, returning in time for tea. We were ready for 5 o/c but the launch did not come till 7.15 for us & our luggage, we were at dinner & so did not go on till 8pm. No one recd us on the 'G.C.' except the stewardess & we were put into one of the Officers wards of 14 beds.

9th SEPTEMBER – Went to Ras-el-Tin, saw S.Bodie who looked very poorly. We went into town, did a little shopping, had lunch & retd to the 'G.C.' after tea. I went with 3 of my Sisters for a sail, we got a nice wetting, but thoroughly enjoyed it. We went to salute our 'Ionian' friends, found the gangway up & a tug near, there was great shouting & cheering from our old friends. After much tacking we retd to our new ship to watch & greet the 'Ionian' friends as they steamed past with her 3,000 troops & 97 Officers & wish them God speed. Our orders were to rejoin her, the boat, at Lemnos. The 'G.Castle' is going tomorrow evening.

10th SEPTEMBER – Left Alex. at 5 o/c in the aft. The sea was rather lively, several Sisters & Officers were not so in consequence of it. Capt Clewes or (…?…) is the Commander of the ship – said to be pro German & in front of some Off. & men said "thank God I am not English". They are watching & waiting to get something more definite. We were all put in one of the Officers wards (10 of us) the others in rows of 3 & myself to the smaller half.

11th SEPTEMBER – Sea still lively, did some ironing, but feeling very tired. Rested a good part of the day.

12th SEPTEMBER – Sea not rough as we are now in the Aegean Sea, among the islands. Cannot reach Mudros before the boom is closed so are slowing down to arrive early tomorrow morning. Had an early morning service at which we were 6 of us, 2 Officers & 2 men. Had a later service at 10.45am, very good service & well attended by all.

13th SEPTEMBER – Arrived in harbour, the torpedoed 'Southlands' alongside. Went on board the 'Simla' after lunch. The 'Ionian' still had her troops on board, we were very pleased to find she had arrived safe & sound.

14th SEPTEMBER – She, (the 'Ionian') disembarked most of her troops, we watched from the 'Simla'.

15th SEPTEMBER – Still a few troops disembarked from 'Ionian'. 11am recd orders to be ready to join 'Ionian' in the afternoon, baggage to be ready by 1pm. All ready but at 2.30pm recd word that the orders were cancelled. At the same time orders had been recd on board the 'Ionian' that she was having over 500 pts to take to England in the afternoon. The Officers & men hurried on well with the cleaning & preparations for the wounded & then got orders to pack up all stores & their own things & be off by 6.30pm. The ship was wanted for other purposes, so the whole staff came along here, & now are on board.

16th SEPTEMBER – Very cold day & stormy.

17th SEPTEMBER – Stores, med & Red X, to be given over to the ship for use of the 'S.S. Northland'.

18th SEPTEMBER – Staff of M.O.'s Sisters & R.A.M.C. went on board the 'Cornwallis' to a concert. Went over the ship with the Lt Commander, he gave me a set of Turkish bullets. I moved one of the guns about. Left for 'S.S. Northland' with all our comforts etc. for our wounded.

19th SEPTEMBER – 'Valdivia' alongside with wounded. Captn Bennett made O/C of 'S.S.Simla' & with myself & staff, received 401 wounded & sick patients from the 'Valdivia' Hosp. ship to be taken to Alex. The 7 Sisters of the 'Nile' staff & 8 of the 'Baltana', to accompany us to Alex to fetch their kits & all the staff, including ourselves, to return as soon as possible, by orders of Sir James Porter. We left Mudros same evening about 5pm. Ship (wards) very dirty.

20th SEPTEMBER – Some of the patients very ill, one poor boy had to have inj. Antitoxin (dip). There are 32 Officers & 2 W.O.'s. Had floors thoroughly scrubbed & lots of dirty linen turned out.

21st SEPTEMBER – Improvement in the condition of most patients, others not so well, the dip a slight improvement. Near the spot where a troop ship was sunk yesterday – the Captn having recd a wireless message of the same & a warning to keep a sharp look out. Yesterday 2 or 300 miles out of our course, so we do not reach Alex so soon. Ship going about 10 knots an hour, but during last night, or early morning (about 2am) she seemed to increase her speed very much (maybe on receipt of wireless). Four Sisters relieved for 2 hrs yesterday & 5 today. Sister Mc helped do the dressings in 2 lower. A submarine sunk a troop ship (thought to be Italian ship) a submarine sighted by our Captain (Jenkins) & Officers (on the bridge) at noon, but disappeared.

22nd SEPTEMBER – Patient died 'hyperpyrexia' (shewing signs of cerebro spinal), he was buried the same morning at sea. A chaplain, who was a patient, reading the burial service.

23rd SEPTEMBER – Arrived at Alex & went into dock on 44 quay at 9am. All 401 patients disembarked before 1pm, many going to Cairo, most Officers to Alex. The 15 Sisters (passengers) to go to the Grand for duty. We were all warned to leave the 'Simla' for the 'Formosa' to return to Lemnos for duty on ship.

24th SEPTEMBER – Went to the 'Formosa', took our luggage, had lunch, then informed we were to return to the 'Simla' for the night, as the 'Simla' was not disinfected after the patients, although they had been 3 days without patients. We retd to the 'Simla', went out after tea, saw Captn Anderson who had come on as O/C in the 'Orsova' Orient Line. He invited us round after dinner. We accepted the invitation. I went to see Commander Coad (the Captain) who invited us all in. They were going to Australia for troops.

25th SEPTEMBER – Left the 'Simla' for the Khedivial Palace Hotel. I then went to see Miss Oram & was told to hold myself in readiness with Sister Cooper & 4 other Q.A.I.M.N.S.R. (of whom I was to be the head) to embark on the 'Evani', a South African Hosp. ship, with a Matron & 4 Sisters from there. I am to assist getting things in order & see how things are. 5 of my former staff to go to No. 15, 2 to go to Cairo (the Australian), Miss Miller (New Zealand) to go to 'Galeka' Hosp. ship. Bodey came to see me in the evening. After dinner helped Miss Wilson to arrange about baggage lists. 100 V.A.D. members just arrived. 100 went to Cairo.

26th SEPTEMBER – Helped sort the letters for pigeon holes, not finished in time for church. Miss Miller not fit to go to *'Galeka'* she is to stay in bed on a milk diet. This was previously near the Khedivial Palace Hotel. I am told it is colossal, rooms very lofty, walls of halls & saloons of marble, some of the ceilings have very decent pictures. Went to church in the evening, a very good service & sermon but I felt too poorly to enjoy it. Saw Thomas & Jones & 2 or 3 others.

27th SEPTEMBER – Had passed a very bad night feeling dreadfully ill, up most of the night vomiting & diarrhoea & in great pain & 2 or 3 times very nearly collapsed, the Sister with me getting rather alarmed. Dr (Captn Bicker) man came to see me at 9.30 & said I was not to get out of bed at all & to be kept on water & santa med. bism. & chlorodyne. S.Miller taken to Sister's Hospital with typhoid. Bodey came.

28th SEPTEMBER – Abdominal pains easier no diar or sickness. Captn came at 10am, said I must still keep to my bed but might have a little milk pudding & bread & butter, milk or tea. Just a little sick after the pudding & very little after the toast. Everyone very kind & had some lovely roses from I.G.Smith. Up 2 hrs.

29th SEPTEMBER – Temp. 99°.

30th SEPTEMBER – Dr.(Captn Washer) came & ordered me to the Sister's Hospital, went in the afternoon. Lt Gumner examined me, said my spleen was enlarged very much. I had to stay in bed, not get out for anything & keep to fluids. Had Brom. 2 doses, but after that still a fair amount of pain, had hot water bottle & a blanket, easier, slept fairly well till awakened for dose of castor oil, no sleep after as the oil & I kept up a continual fight. I won sufficiently, though not altogether. Had toast, beef tea & a little pudding for lunch, sick a little after.

1st OCTOBER – Had castor oil early morning, with good result & much pain.

2nd OCTOBER – Had a better night & less pain.

3rd OCTOBER – Good night, pain once or twice only.

4th OCTOBER – Got up for tea, not allowed in garden.

5th OCTOBER – Went for a drive in Aracia, went to Ras-el-Tin, arrived back at 8.30am.

6th OCTOBER – Wanted my bed for another Sister who was ill, so went to Aboukir, arrived at station & being four, could not all go in the donkey cart, so two of us went on donkeys. The ground is all loose sand dotted with many date palms & a few fig & prickly pears. There are a sprinkling of houses, stone & plaster (the latter mostly) & then the natives' huts hidden away, the natives here are Bedouins. It is very interesting to watch the camels & donkeys laden with barrels & tins for water, being driven over to get the water.

7th OCTOBER – We breakfasted on the upper balcony where several slept, having their beds out. I booked one for that night, as two Sisters were going away. Rested all morning till 12 o/c then dressed for lunch. In the afternoon, put on my dressing gown & lay down. At 4 o/c the Officers rode over, Captn Duncan in charge of our escort, bringing 2 small open ambulances to take us for tea to their camp, where we had the pipes & band. We thoroughly enjoyed it. Kings Own Scottish Borders & Scottish Fusiliers, about 600 with all the horses & transport. Went to bed at 9pm on the balcony & slept fine (wrote to Bo & Th & sent it to post).

8th OCTOBER – Had bkft in bed on the balcony & enjoyed it, then helped with some boudoir caps. Lazied all morning.

9th OCTOBER – Went to Alex for some things I required from the hotel. Phoned to Ras-el-Tin & was told May Bodey was ill & Matron. Went to see them, Matron rather better, but Bodey's temp was 104° & had been all day in spite of sponging, do not like it, it was 102° previous day. I had a rush to get things I wanted at the hotel & just caught the train by getting on as it started & walking through to a 2nd class. Changed into a 1st with the other Sisters after. Kept awake by dogs most of the night. H. Thomas left Ras-el-Tin & went on ship 'Haverford'.

10th OCTOBER – Dull morning. Had a very good service at 11.30am in the sitting room – Communion service with a short address on 'she hath done what she could', speaking of the loving & with service rendered to our men, for their bravery, but asked was it done as unto Him always, as if Christ was the one being tended & did we use our opportunities. Sr Bodie a shade better. I telephoned. Our Ras-el-Tin orderlies left for Salonika.

11th OCTOBER – Sister Bodey temp still 104°, so was taken to the sick Sisters Hosp. with supposed enteric.

12th OCTOBER – Sr B rather better.

13th OCTOBER – Went for a walk with Sisters Condick & Cornwell, we went along the sand close to the sea, the only easy walking, till the 3rd hill, then crossed & came back behind the Bedouin camp where we took some snap shots. Felt very tired, having to sit down 3 or 4 times.

14th OCTOBER – Mother's birthday, wrote father, Sister Bodey better, temp nearly normal 99°, but still vomiting a good deal.

15th OCTOBER – Friday – Went for a horse ride on Charlie, rode astride, very aching ribs after. The horses raced, which took it out of us.

16th OCTOBER – Went for a ride on Daisy, got on better, but very aching ribs & legs (& bruised) did not feel so tired. I had bathed in the morning. Saw Gough & Rice Oclay, who had come out for half days. Heard from Sr Miller.

17th OCTOBER – Lizzie S birthday. I had a swim in deep water but with life belt. Good size mullet swimming all round the house boat.

18th OCTOBER – Saw Mr Gunson at Sick Sisters Hosp. he recommended another week. Went to Nelsons Island (sailed), several Sisters sick, nothing but heather & shrub.

19th OCTOBER – Went for a ride on Daisy again. All the party went a new way exploring, passed round the Khedives Harem, low stone buildings with a stone wall round. Had a swim near the shore.

20th OCTOBER – Went for a swim near the shore, got on very fairly well. In the evening went up by the old Aboukir fort to see the sunrise [sunset].

21st OCTOBER – Had a swim, got on better & kept up longer. Took photos in the Aboukir camp, near the fort.

22nd OCTOBER – Had a bathe only, as S. Birkett upset us, she would swim to shore & called out for succour. I asked 2 men to go to her aid, which they did, only to find she wanted us near in case anything went wrong & insisted on finishing her swim in spite of upsetting us & hindering us all from getting a swim at all.

23rd OCTOBER – Went for a swim but did not feel very well. Several Sisters came & we went to the boathouse.

24th OCTOBER – Went for a walk after going in deep water with life belt.

25th OCTOBER – Went for a swim & at evening went with several others for a long donkey ride, which we thoroughly enjoyed as the donkeys went well, very well cantering & trotting. Went along the Manmondick Canal & back over the desert.

26th OCTOBER – Went for a walk with S.Tyndall to take photos of camp (Bedouin) mine had come out well, also the photos of S. Osborne by the camel in the village & others. I returned to the New Khedivial Hotel, Alex. Bodey came with me for a drive.

27th OCTOBER – On duty for temp – duty to assist Matron Wilson in the hotel. I felt very tired, legs especially, at the evening of the day!

28th OCTOBER – Had a rather tiring day.

29th OCTOBER – I received last evening a letter of enquiry from the War Office, re a patient Driver Barfield F.Amb. R.A.M.C. concerning £30 – 35 which he said (while he was a pt on the 'H.S.Gondola') that he had given to the Sister O/C of his ward on 'Ionian' to keep for him & it had not been transferred with him. Made enquiries but as no one remembered him & all valuables were given to the O/C at once. He was very ill & we concluded did not know what he was saying.
  Bodey came to see me (not looking so well) Sister Hawken, a N.Z. Sister died during the night & was buried this afternoon. A transport torpedoed with staff of N.Z. Sisters on board, also Drs & R.A.M.C. men & many troops (no particulars of the saved) but hear that most are saved, hope it is so (said to be going to Salonika).

30th OCTOBER – While an ambulance bringing the Sisters from the schools (attached to 19 G.Hosp) to lunch, it was dashed into by an express. One Sister (Griffiths, Res.) was killed, the driver & 2 Sisters unconscious, one of the latter, Cavanagh, having her arm broken & head cut, also eye injured, several were badly shaken. The one who was killed saw the express coming, jumped out, called to the others & helped them out, then ran round to help those on the front with the driver. They seem stupefied, however she got Hollows down & was pulling Cavanagh down when she met her death. The gates were open, the man beckoned them across, but a mule stuck & would not go on, or, possibly they might have just cleared, but it is doubtful. A V.A.D. died same night, named Roskell (Bodie & I had a drink).

31st OCTOBER – Sister Griffiths & Mrs Roskell buried at 4 o/c. I went to St Marks in the morning, very busy after.

1st NOVEMBER – They arrived in Alex harbour with the survivors of the 'Marquette' on board, there were 20 Sisters, 10 were lost, some fell exhausted, they were 7 hrs in the water. Some were lost through another boat being lowered on top of them. 4 out of the survivors were on the boat too ill to be moved, the other 16 went to the Grand Hotel. Grigor, who was on the 'Galeka' with us, is not one of those very ill. All New Zealanders, the lost were (…?…) (some have been recovered but, except for the discs, were unrecognisable).

6th NOVEMBER – Heard Kitchener had been in Alex previous Monday or Tuesday (3rd or 9th) & had gone to the peninsula. Miss Oram (Matron in Chief of Egypt) also went up for the inspection. 27th, 28th & 29th Gen Hosp. started (previously only the 18th & Australian) in Mudros.

8th NOVEMBER – Mr Kent died. Met Col. Mayo Robson again.

23rd NOVEMBER – Sent my book of photos home by Miss Oakley on H.S.

24th NOVEMBER – Capt Gillis called, heard that Captn Henry had gone to Canada for a rest but was returning to Egypt shortly. He left the 'Ionian' to go to Canada. Captn Williams now on 'Ionian', Gillis still on the 'Tunisian'.

25th or 26th NOVEMBER – Sent album home by Sr Oakley.

30th NOVEMBER – Bodie retd to duty to Ras-el-Tin.

DECEMBER – 'S.S.Persia' torpedoed, many lives lost & all our xmas mail, parcels etc.

2nd DECEMBER – Went to Dartons to supper. Heard that Kitchener had done away with the 'Aragon' (that noted vessel for luxury, contradictory orders & for not getting what you wanted, luxury. When Sisters, Officers & men were going short of necessities on land). Hurrah for Kitchener. Australian force to go to the border of Tripoli, trouble with the Bedouins there. (Sent parcels for Nellie to Sr Hobbes).

4th DECEMBER – Miss Wilson left for Cairo, leaving me in temp. charge of Khedivial Hotel.

5th DECEMBER – 5 Sisters reported sick & put in sick room.

8th DECEMBER – Sister Hebbert removed to Sick Sisters Hosp, enteric.

10th DECEMBER – Sister O'Pearson & Miss Gilham remd to Sick Sisters Hosp, enteric.

11th DECEMBER – Miss Wilson returned from Cairo & a number of Sisters from Cairo for 19th Stationary, Imbros & some for Salonika. 6 of ours left same day for Salonika & a number of Sisters from the Grand for Imbros, also a few of those 100 who came out yesterday from England left for these places. Sent cigarettes & sweets to Thomas for himself & other B'ham men.

12th DECEMBER – Sunday – Had bkft in bed, wrote letters on the terrace in the morning. Very hot today. Went to church in the evening, 20 minutes before time, but could not get in at all, even for standing, so had to return.

14th DECEMBER – Moved into our new Post Office, much lighter & more airy, but noisy & dusty, being on the high road, where there is so much traffic. Mail came in, 7 days late, a large number of troops have come in & gone out.

16th DECEMBER – Heard of a rising on about the 10th on the Tripoli frontier (among the Bedouins) some of our Officers (3) & 19 men killed.

18th DECEMBER – More Sisters arrived. Have now the list of 15th, 16th, 18th Stationary Hosp. at Mudros. The 1st – 2 at East & the latter at West Mudros, the 19th Stat. at Imbros. The 28th at Salonika, the 29th at Cairo & Alex. All these letters, parcels, papers are to be sent off to them, which makes us busy in the Post Office. Felt almost demented with tiredness, so much to do.

19th DECEMBER – Having morning off, am spending it in bed writing & resting. Went to church.

24th DECEMBER – Christmas tree given to us by the managers, we all had a present from it, mine being a purse. We had a very good band playing to us during dinner. Stayed up till nearly 1am reckoning the money collected & portioning for servants.

25th DECEMBER – Had several presents, brass flowers pots (2), brass & enamel pot, 1 card case, clock, letter holder, brooch, lace (Maltese), box of chocolates, flowers, 2 purses. Sr.Miller & I went to visit the wards at the Oswa El Woska School & see the patients enjoying themselves. The wards were prettily decorated, most of them had Xmas trees, several pianos & the men were playing & singing. Gifts were given from the trees & concerts held in several wards. All had had gifts.

26th DECEMBER – Had a cold so had my morning off & breakfast in bed, went to church & after lunch, for a drive. We had a real Xmas lunch & dinner. The dinner, a wonderful affair, quite a triumph for all concerned. When the time came for the pudding, all lights were put out, then the Chef appeared with a big pudding all ablaze & after him came all the waiters, gliding swiftly & quietly in, each with a blazing pudding. It was a pretty sight & greatly applauded. Cheers were called for the manager & chef. Miss Oram came for the 2nd dinner. We presented the manager with a silver inkstand & tray & the asst. with a silver card case.

28th DECEMBER – Miss Oram's & Miss Wilson's 'At Home' for the staff at our hotel & their friends, each permitted to invite a friend. There was a fairly good concert & refreshment.

29th DECEMBER – Invited to dinner & concert at the Military Hosp. Ras-el-Tin, but hearing in the evening I could go to Cairo for a few days, I begged to be excused as there were several things to see to in the office before I went, the train going at 9am. Miss Oram also had been invited but she had to go to attend a meeting about a place for a nurses club in Alex & so excused herself.

30th DECEMBER – Left at 9am. Miss Palin, my friend Miss M.G.Thomas & 2 others joined at Sidi Gaba Junc & joined their party. The country is well cultivated all the way up & very flat till we reach Cairo. There are the different mounts & forts round. We arrived for lunch & were quite ready for it. After lunch we went to the bazaar, which was most interesting, some of the old houses showing what wonderful work & art they put to the fronts, they were curious old places. We saw the brass workers & were very interested in the busy bazaar. Afterwards we went to the Citadel to see the Mohamed Ali Mosque. It is a great height above the town. The Mosque is very fine & its 2 minarets are 200 – 300 ft high. One enters first a fine courtyard (after being encased in slippers, huge ones). In the centre of yard is a large fountain with marble trench, here the men prepare for their prayers by washing head, hands & feet. On one side is a fine clock presented by Napoleon. The Mosque is of marble white ripening to yellow. The lights from the window are very pretty colours. The ceiling is very fine in gilt & some colour, representing sun & other things. There are about 200 lights, marvellous chandeliers presented by Napoleon in exchange for some marble statues. There is the tomb of (...?...) with the 1st holy carpet of blue silk & gold embroidery over his tomb, 4 angels, 1 at each corner, in brass. The throne for the high priests is very high, about 20 steps up, & is in blue & gold cedarwood. The pulpit of the same, but low. The carpet on the floor is scarlet Persian, with several designs of Solomon Seal & of the rising sun. All round the Mosque is a small gallery, its banister or front of the usual pattern of Cairo woodwork. From the other side of the Mosque runs a balcony from which a very fine view of Cairo can be seen.

31st DECEMBER – We went to the pyramids, in the train to terminus & then on camels. Had our photos taken on the camels as we sat in front of the sphinx. It was a wonderful antiquity, it used to be buried in sand up to the neck, but is now cleared & so the rock bust stands forth. The pyramids are ordinary sandstone encased in marble. We climbed up the largest, taking 25 minutes to go up, the Arabs helping us up, 10 minutes to come down. At the foot of the 2nd we had lunch & very glad we were to get it. After lunch we went inside the pyramid, but I was glad to get out. The view from the pyramids is very fine. I took a photo of the Sisters on the top. We were very hot & tired. We arrived back at the Continental 4.30, had a bath & then went down for tea. After tea went out to the shops. Just as we were going out about 40 soldiers were ushered in, passed through to the garden. On enquiry learnt that a large number of Australians, coming from the peninsulas, were furious because the bars at this hotel & Shepherds were closed to them at a certain hour & so they threatened to burn them. Sounds exciting for us. Met Miss Kirk from Rome (S.C.R.E.) we were surprised. After dinner the mounted troops were out, about 200 – 300 going backwards & forwards, as well as the Infantry picket. These kept guard all night.

Original photograph of Katy (2nd left) and party taken at the Sphinx.

1916

1st JANUARY – After breakfast the 5 of us drove out to see the old Cairo. The 1st Copt Church, ancient Greek & the church built over the cave, where Joseph & Mary rested with the babe on their flight through Egypt, a very fine old crypt, the church above had some fine carving & pictures & tapestry, but all dirty & neglected. The priest took us round, men were busy repairing, carpenters etc. In all their churches are 3 altars, the frontispieces were put on one side. The oldest church was filthy, one could imagine what it would look like when clean, which it had not done for many, many years. The streets were of the narrowest & so interlaced, one could not find the way without a guide. To enter the city, we had to go down a steep place to what looked like a hole 15 – 20ft down. Here you came to an old door of wood, rough, but very, very strong & thick, the bolts of wood like a beam going into the wall, both door & walls were Roman. A high wall surrounded the city. We went round to see the gate of Babylon, a huge old iron barred gate so where they entered when they took the city. We crossed the Nile to the island of Rhoda, where are big harems of Pascha (…?…). Seeing some of the daughters, our guide instantly covered his face with my camera case, but the girls bade us come forward, asked if we would like some coffee, took us to see one of their harems. Every room very lofty, spacious & clean (their own home). They were high class Egyptian, their father & mother well. A young girl friend living with them spoke English & acted as interpreter. She, with the 2 girls dressed in black European style, took us in the drawing room, an immense room, but not quite so large as the dining room, on the floor a beautiful Persian carpet. The furniture all encased in white, a few ornaments about, a bookcase full of French & Egyptian books & a few English. Some of the furniture was very fine inlaid cedar, ebony & ivory. The ceilings of these two rooms were very fine, but this house was only 80 yrs old. We went into the bedroom where we found an ordinary brass bed & fittings, toilet tables, a large flat desk (very modern) & chairs & couch, but no fittings on the dressing table as we would have. Instead a lot of frames covered with hair, very high, which they put on before their head coverings (only high cast allowed to wear these). In the dining room was an old grandfather clock, a fine mahogany one inlaid. In the (…?…) church was a painting of the Virgin Mary & Child (name of painter unknown) whose eyes were splendidly done, the eyes following one in every position. We spent a most interesting morning & returned back to the hotel for lunch. After lunch we drove to the (…?…) Mosque, a very fine old place. The courtyard in excellent condition, walls & chapels towering above us of alabaster from the pyramids, the many lanterns or lamps had been removed to the museum as it is now only used by visitors, no services being held there. In the centre a huge canopy over the usual fountains for ablutions no longer needed. The interior must have been very fine before it was despoiled by the Egyptian government, who stripped the gold leaf from the ceilings, (in the Coptic churches were good old Coptic bibles, good condition). (High upon the outside of the walls was a cannon ball lodged & many holes made by them, shot by Napoleon's men who rushed the Citadel) & walls, leaving a little here & there to show what it had been like. There is a coronation chair of cedar, ebony & ivory & other woods, all dovetailed & very fine inlaid altar, a great ugly barricade of wood surrounding the tomb of (…?…) in the centre marring the whole. We afterwards went to the museum, where I should like to have spent more time. It is a very fine building containing some fine old relics of all sorts, but one visit was such a short one as we had to return to the hotel for tea, settle our bills & be ready to leave Cairo by the 6.35pm train. Miss Wilson welcomed me back & had placed some lovely roses in my room. Just as we entered a knock came from my next door neighbour, Sister Wood, so Miss W. said laughingly, "you must go to show yourself".

2nd JANUARY – Had an early visit from my asst. Sister Miller to welcome me back. My breakfast was brought up by Mohammed, who seemed pleased to see me back. I went to write letters & then to church. It is my morning off.

4th JANUARY – Our men evacuated the peninsula with one man killed (but afterwards we heard there were nearly 100 killed & wounded). Our men burning the stores & setting old guns in the trenches, to the triggers of which were 2 cans, so arranged that one full of water gradually emptied itself into the other & when the 2nd was full it released the trigger & off went the guns. They were fixed for varied times, thus making the Turks think they had not evacuated the trenches. Many of the Australians were naturally very much upset at leaving the place where so many of their brave brothers had given up their lives to obtain for their country & feeling was very bitter. I think, had Churchill been anywhere near, he could not have been saved, whatever he denied. Many of these men were already up in Cairo when I was there & these thoughts made them so daring & get out of hand. Very many were sent straight up to the fighting line again, near the Suez, with our own boys. For many days we had men & stores passing the hotel, in hundreds. On the 6th, 7th & 8th they were constantly passing to the various camps.

8th JANUARY – Went to Darton's to find out if Joe was on the 'Persia' which had been torpedoed, but found she had been unable to obtain a berth, so her father cabled to her & Mr & Mrs Ross not to come till the journey was safer.

9th JANUARY – Thousands of troops paraded in Alex purposely, I suppose, to show the natives we could keep them under, as the Bedouins were being very troublesome round.

11th JANUARY – Had a very exciting night. Two of our nurses came to me at 10.20pm (while I was waiting for a Sister to return from Cairo) saying that one of the nurses had been shut in the bathroom for ¾ hr when she called to her, knocked

& could get no reply. After ¼ hr, hearing no sign, she reported it. I went upstairs, called, knocked gently, then louder, but could not hear a sound, so ran down, got the night porter, who tried to break open the door, but could not, although he tried in various ways. I tried to get the duplicate key, but could not. I got the manager still they could not force the door. I went for a strong knife to try the lock, thinking we must get the lock picked. When I arrived again at the door, she calmly unlocked it & walked out, bidding the men & everyone go out. We all knew she had a bad head. I had to put a Sister on duty as special with her. Her pulse was quite good. It seemed to be hysterical temper, bordering on insanity. We got her to Sick Sisters next evening, where she was watched constantly. Hearing, they had decided to send her home (as mentally unfit) she desired to have her discharge here, but of course, they would not permit that. She declared she would stay, however she was guarded too well & embarked on 24th for England with Sister Galbraith who refused responsibility, though she promised to do what she could with her.

13th JANUARY – Had a restless night & when I arose at 6 o/c had violent pain, followed by diarrhoea, succeeded in dressing as it was my morning to see the Sisters off to their various hospitals, managed to see the first lot off then Miss Wilson came & ordered me to bed. In bed quite easy & the attacks of pain etc stopped. Was put in the sick room for that evening.

14th JANUARY – Pain came on again next morning (the colon). So Dr insisted that I must go to Sick Sisters Hosp. so I was placed on a stretcher & taken in an ambulance. Had a very disturbed night.

15th JANUARY – Next morning was very tired. A little more comfortable. Mrs Bell (Aus. Dr) brought in with influenza & put in the little ward with me. Her husband also Dr (Aus.) at 19th.

16th JANUARY – Sunday – From 9 – 12 I had 3 hrs constant pain, like bad, very acute neuralgia in the colon, till the tears forced themselves down my cheeks. It went easy after & although I still had much flatulence etc I did not get real bad pain again. Miss Wilson came to see me, also Miss Miller, one bringing books & the latter flowers & Eau de Cologne.

18th JANUARY – Miss Wilson came to see me, feeling better.

19th JANUARY – Miller came & had tea with me.

20th JANUARY – Bodey came bringing flowers & magazines. Got up for tea & then back to bed again.

21st JANUARY – Got up for tea, Thomson came, had tea with me & stayed for some time. Stayed up for dinner at 7, very cold, caught cold.

22nd JANUARY – Came to Conval.[convalescent] Home Zizinia, where were 15 others. Went on the beach after lunch, rested, but was very pleased when bedtime came. Had various visitors to see me next few days & soon began to feel better in spite of the stormy days, rain & hurricanes. Tents went down on the night of the 25th like nine pins in the camps near, roofs, whole & in part, were blown off the hospitals & houses & one hut carried on to the train lines. The new Victoria Hotel (a large red building) situated above the beach here on the highest point for miles around, lost many of its letters on the roof & the rest were twisted about in all directions. This commands a view over Alex even the harbour & bay, & I should think, with powerful glasses, any ship could be seen leaving the harbour & could be signalled out to the enemy at a good distance. It was here about 16 days ago, that the manager then dressed as an English Staff Officer, was caught signalling. He was shot & rumour says another also, of that I am not sure. The place is now closed, everyone was told to go. There is now by day & night a policeman above & one on the beach guarding it, as there are steps right down to the beach. Miss Willoughby (a Canadian Matron staying here from Cairo) & I generally mount these steps & watch the sunset & after glow from the top as we get such a view from there. Of course, we cannot go inside the wall & he does not allow others than the Sisters to do even that.

25th JANUARY – All here went to Grand Entertainment at the Alhambra, funds for the recreation room for the men.

27th JANUARY – Thomson came to wish me goodbye, as she was off with the 29th G.H. for Salonica on the morrow. Reported to Dr, who said I was to stay another week (Saturday).

28th JANUARY – The 29th composed of some of the original 29th, some of 21st – & 20th G.H. left for Salonica. Bodey came to see me.

30th JANUARY – Went to All Saints, Bulkley, in the morning, had a rather warm walk back. The service was very bright.

31st JANUARY – Miss Crews (V.A.D.) left. Her home is at Exmouth, she is invalided home after jaundice, very sick about it. Is to go on Feb 4th. I find she knows several of my old friends & acquaintances there.

1st FEBRUARY – Went with Miss Bertha Willoughby to Mex, about 2/3rds of the way there, we were held up nearly an hour, because the previous tram had run over a Syrian boy. There were crowds of people (natives) round (jabbering away) also police, altogether about 12 officials. Eventually the Captn came examined the car, had the 2nd unhinged, examined that, took particulars & sent us on. The boy had been taken at once by an English Officer, coming by in a motor, to the hospital. Do not know if he died. We arrived at Mex too late to see the place.

2nd FEBRUARY – Went for a motor run, the car lent by the Red X. We went along the old Cairo Rd by the side of the Mamoudick Canal, were out 2 hrs, passed many mud villages, everywhere there were pretty busy with agriculture, cotton, grain & vegetables. The Canal was a very busy scene, so many huge cargoes of cotton. They pack their boats so high. The groups of cattle were very curious in some places, all near together, you would see camels, buffaloes, donkeys, sheep, goats & mules, the horses ought to have been shot, they looked every moment as if they must fall, so thin & their legs bent, it was pitiful. We returned round by the salt lake, the wind rather cold, but we had a most enjoyable run. Miss Wilson came to see me in the afternoon & to meet Mrs Burleigh & Mrs Richmond – both very energetic & practical Red Cross ladies.

3rd FEBRUARY – Feeling rather tired, am resting in bed rather later. It is a beautiful morning. Heard our men marching past, whistling as usual. They pass the end of our street every day to & from the camps. We had 10 men & a Corporal from the small convalescent camp to tea. After tea Bodey, Willoughby & I went for cigarettes for them. They had various games & the gramophone, songs & recitations, men & Sisters taking part. They seemed quite sorry when time for their departure arrived.

7th FEBRUARY – Miss Fordham said a friend of hers, Mrs Camplin, would have 4 of us to lunch & tea. We left at 12.15pm, walked to the train, went by train to Victoria, then took a train to Mamourch Street. Here we were met by a native who conducted us down the line a short distance to where a trolley awaited us to convey us to the house. It was a strange carriage we were highly amused. It was

 drawn by a mule & ran on lines which were most uneven, over a narrow uneven muddy road, with very wide ditches on either side, one side dirty water, the other clean. These roads were about 1 or 2 acres apart. The whole estate had been reclaimed land from an old salt lake, had been bought by a syndicate for cultivation. It was 30 – 40,000 acres. Mr Camplin was one of the heads, of which there were several, 6 having volunteered for the war. The old chairman had come out to help superintend while they were away. There were several native mud villages where the native workers lived. There was also a house built by a German who had bought a small piece of land, but was not living there now. (Even on this isolated portion they had made their plans). It took us 35 minutes, although the mule went well, to arrive at our destination. Our hostess, a bright, smart little lady came out to welcome us. The house stood in the middle of the lawns & flower gardens, where sweet peas were just commencing to bloom. The house looked very homey inside & out, was well appointed & very tastefully furnished. It seemed, in many ways, as if we had suddenly stepped out of Egypt into a comfortable English home, except for the Arab servants in their usual white robes, red turban, slippers & sashes. After lunch we went into the garden, where most English vegetables & many Eastern were growing. Mrs Camplin was very proud of her English parsley (the parsley here is like the Italian, not curly, open flat leaves). There were a good number of Cape gooseberry trees, the fruit has an outer shell like the Japanese lantern, but when the fruit is ripe the outer part is yellow, not red. We brought a basketful away with us, which next morning, were greatly appreciated by the Sisters at breakfast time. There was a male palm (date) in flower, the flower very like a huge pampas flower only thicker. They take the pollen & put it on the female palm to make them more fruitful. The bananas, which were nearly finished, were very good. They had about 20 English fowl, but found the half breeds lay best. There were also turkeys & ducks. After tea we had to start on our return journey, on the way back we met Mr W (the chairman) in his trolley, they lifted his trolley off the lines for us to pass & once we came to a trolley load of berheem, which they pushed back to a siding near. We had a very enjoyable day. Before sowing a fresh crop they flood the land with fresh water, then this soaks through, carrying salt & other matter with it, into these ditches which are run off. They grow cotton, grain, vegetables, fruit & berheems (clover) of this latter they get 3 crops by cutting it 3 times in succession.

8th FEBRUARY – Miss Willoughby left us for Cairo, feeling much better for her stay here. She was feeling sad over the death of Col. Duff C.R.A.M.C. who had died that morning & who had been very kind to her. Miss Oram went by the same train, was in it when it arrived at Sidi Gaba. She said she was pleased to see me so much better. When I retn I was to see Miss W went away for a holiday.

9th FEBRUARY – Reported to Dr who wished me to stay till 14th, though I was much better.

11th FEBRUARY – Sr Miller & Miss Radcliffe came to see me, met on the beach, about 3.45 went to Saba Pacha for tea at Mr Andersons. He has lent his house for the use of the Sisters & we can take anyone we like to tea for 4 piastres [currency: Egyptian £] & go into the garden, play tennis or croquet. While there I saw in the garden a very peculiar palm flower about ¾ yard in circumference, on top of the palm, which was about 3ft high, the petals were something the shape of an oak leaf, brown, thick & velvety, they were piled thick one on top of the other & in between, here & there, could be seen what looked at 1st like smooth strawberries, which were also very profuse, they were so pretty. After tea we went to see the little church & then down on to the rocks, watching from thence the native fishermen & the lovely sunset. In the evening 5 of us went to see the Pops, which was good.

12th & 13th FEBRUARY – Rested on the beach most of the time.

14th FEBRUARY – Returned to the Khedivial Hotel, went to tea with Mrs Nora Darton at Mustapha. Had a letter from Sis in which I heard the War Office had wired me.

15th FEBRUARY – Started duty again at the Khedivial, found the 1st few days rather trying.

18th FEBRUARY – saw Lt Brown, one of our 'Ionian' M.O.'s, heard from him that Captn Bennett had gone home 'nephritis', Cptn Anderson had para. ty, Lt Garrad, Allan & King all well & sent to various places.

20th FEBRUARY – I had a busy morning, then went to the Darton's for the rest of the day.

21st FEBRUARY – Miss Wilson went to Cairo from 18th – 21st, returned for the opening of the Nurses Club next day at 4 o/c.

22nd FEBRUARY – Spent my off duty time with Bodey, had tea out.

23rd FEBRUARY – Went to Victoria on train with Miller.

24th FEBRUARY – Called on Mrs Bell who is at Cairo till 1st March.

25th FEBRUARY – Had a day off, went to Ras-el-Tin for tea & lunch. Had a hot water bag given me.

26th FEBRUARY – Joined the Nurses Club, Alex, had tea with Miss Bond there. On my return at 6 o/c learnt that the General Commanding had issued an order to all Officers & Sister to return at once to their qrs. Phone messages sent to the Khedivial to all hospitals & clubs to that effect. The tram cars were stopped & all sent back to their respective qrs. None were to go out that day again. The 'Ebani' put out without several Officers & Sisters, who were on shore when the order came for her to go, so we were told to put the Sisters up. I waited till 11.30 then went to bed as they did not come. Reported that Austrian war ships were outside (off Alex). A large store at the docks & a ship were on fire (I hear destroyed) 'S.S. Hunt's Green'.

27th FEBRUARY – Went to church, found another order had been sent forth that everyone was to be in their qrs by 8pm & none to go out after. Just heard it was the 'S.S. Hunt's Green' who was on fire last night, she has a large store of petrol on board. Do not know how it got alight. The store was said to be done by natives.

8th MARCH – Sent Howard £80 to invest for me.

10th MARCH – The 'H.S.Rasheed' brought 91 sick & wounded, mostly the latter & among them the 2nd leader of the enemies on the Western Frontier, as prisoner the head one was killed. The previous journey they had taken Sister Humfries & the rest of the Sisters (16th Stationary Hosp) to Maraah Matru as a clearing station.

19th MARCH – The 'Rasheen' brought men & women who had been rescued from the Bedouins. These had been wrecked on the (…?…) & taken prisoners (about 40 I think), there are still more as prisoners who have been taken further inland.

23rd MARCH – Miss Taylor, my chief Asst left, she sailed with about 80 other V.A.D.'s (among who were Joyce & Mrs Parkes) on the *'Dunluce Castle'*. We went down to see them on board. They steamed out at about 5 o/c. Captn Miles (Sam's friend) came to see me. I liked him very much & wished I could have seen more of him, but I had promised to see the girls off & he was going to France with his division (6th) & so it could not be. After leaving the docks at 2.50 we rode off to Cairo station (Miss Radcliffe & I) to board the train for Montasa, I had a day off & she ½ a day. We took our tea & enjoyed it as we sat on the rocks close to the waters' edge, the sea a lovely blue. I had taken tea in my thermos. The Khedive has a very pretty house there, now used as an Officers convalescent home, the other buildings used formerly by some of his suite, have tents round & are used by the men. An ideal spot in which to convalesce. The sea was lovely & all so very quiet. Troops have been leaving for 2 weeks until scarcely any are left. Sidi Bishr only seems to have A.S.C. all along the Victoria line seems the same, where thousands, many thousands, now only a few hundred remain.

24th MARCH – Again volunteers are asked for Mesopotamia & plenty obtained. The 23rd Stat left on the 19th evening for Suez & then the *'H.S. Assaye'*, presumably for Mesopotamia, Miss Hodgins in charge.

25th MARCH – Miss Wilson going to Luxor, Miss Murphy (Q.S.) Matron to assist me & relieve me. She is from Luxor Convalescent Hospital, which closed on the 13th, the Sisters coming here on the 16th. Heard last night that 15th G.H. is to pack up at once & that there is no longer any Egyptian expeditionary force, only to be garrison, also the Staffords portion of Lord Derby's scheme have arrived here. There is to be one mounted rgt of N.Zealanders & one of (...?...) to guard the canal, & new Australian forces are to come. (Re the prisoners on Western Frontier rescued by the Duke of Westminster's armed cars on 17/ 3/16). A start was made from Sollum 3am with armoured cars (Ford cars) with machine guns, 23 transport cars & 10 motor ambulances. 120 miles were covered before reaching the wells, where the prisoners were, came in sight. The guards to the number of 30 fled to a distance, then opened fire, but were rapidly accounted for & our prisoners supplied with food, the cars were back at Bir Aziza, where an advanced post for the reception of prisoners had been made at 1.30am. Considering the deprivations the prisoners had suffered, their condition is as good as can be expected. 4 died of diseases & wounds since Novr. They were, with these exceptions, brought back in *'H.S. Rasheed'*. Two of them an Officer & an interpreter were away from the camp 2 days previous to the rescue, to assist in obtaining food & clothing for the rest. Good hopes are entertained of their recovery. The Turkish & Arab Officers treated them with consideration, the hardness of their lot was due to lack of food, raiment & med. comforts than maltreatment.

Miss Wilson gone to Luxor & Assouan.

26th MARCH – The Officer & interpreter (prisoners in Bedouin camp, Western Frontier) rescued & taken to Tripoli, Italian territory. Coal in Alexandria is now 150/- per ton.

27th MARCH – 8 fresh Sisters arrived from home on the 'Esequivo' they were Sisters off boats which had been disbanded & who had been home on sick leave.

28th MARCH – Quite hot, no breeze. Went for a walk through Egyptian Hosp. Rue Rosette Gdns past El Woska Schools, down to the water works & back by the sea.

29th MARCH – More details come from home, wrote to Dennis Smith, gun practice at fortifications. Sultry day, showers in the afternoon. Miss W left Luxor for Assouan. Heard from father of Wm Hyde's sudden death. Gun practice was between Port Kaid Bay & Glymenopoulo (sea coast).

30th MARCH – Dennis Smith came to see me, he is like his father in features, but fair – seems a nice boy. He was on the peninsula from July – Septr when he had a slight wound & dysentery. When better he was attached to the naval signalling section on Imbros till after the evacuation in Febry, when he came to Sidi Bishr, hoping to rejoin his regt (9th Roy Warwicks). We went for a walk & had dinner together.

3rd APRIL – Rev McInnes – Bishop of Jerusalem, called at the K.H. to see a friend. He asked me various questions about the hotel, chatted a while, then shook hands & departed. He gave some very interesting lectures on old Cairo & on Gen Gordon, I could not go to either.

7th APRIL – Miss Radcliffe & Mrs Watson, my remaining 2 V.A.D.'s, left me for England on H.S. 'Dunluce Castle' Dennis came to say goodbye, so went with me to see the V.A.D. members off. He & I afterwards, went to Darton's to dinner, he enjoyed 2 games of billiards with Mr Harley.

8th APRIL – Dennis left & I wrote Jack & Sally. He expected to join his regt in Mesopotamia. Sis M.S.Stuart came to help me.

9th APRIL – Went to Ras-el-Tin to chat to Miss Bond & Bodie. Miss Oram said I might go on a ship again later if I wished, but to think it over.

10th APRIL – Sister Foley came to assist in the office instead of M.S.Stuart, who left for 31 Caen Hosp, Port Said. Sis Miller & I went to see the Prince of Wales inspect troops & camps at Sidi Bishr, but he did not go, only General Murray, but we enjoyed the afternoon. It was a cold wind.

11th APRIL – H.S. 'Delta' sails with the renowned Mrs Waldron on board. She was the famous Mrs Richard Chamberlain, the renowned lady of South Africa:

'There was a young lady of Berwick
Whose conduct was highly hysteric
She followed the drums, distributing buns
To the men who were down with enteric'

She had been more abominable in Alex & Cairo, treating the orderlies abominably, even swearing at them. Most of the Sisters, even V.A.D.'s & Officers hated or disliked her (mutton dressed as lamb).

12th APRIL – Very windy & cold.

13th APRIL – Very stormy wind & sand so thick, it was like a heavy fog, a khamsin such as this, the weal papers say, has never been known. It lasted till about 3pm a heavy sea followed. It was quite warm out & very depressing. The strong wind & heavy seas continued through the night.

14th APRIL – Sister S.G.Butler was drowned at Sidi Bishr at the Sprouting rocks. She, with a party of Officers, Sisters & V.A.D.'s, had gone for a picnic to see the spray on the rocks & to take photos of the same. She & one V.A.D. member dismounted from their donkeys, ran on ahead & stood on a high rock to photograph the others coming along. Having her back to the sea she did not notice a huge wave coming in, which took her off her feet & carried her away. The other jumped from it so did not get full force, she tried to clutch Sister but could not reach her. Sister knew it was too late, motioned her back saying "too late", she turned on her back & floating, was carried away. They could do nothing but watch her drown, she floated for nearly 10 minutes as she could not swim, then disappeared. Her body was found next morning several miles away at Moutaza by the Coast Guard, perfectly natural except for a slight bruise on her face & the face quite calm, as I imagine she would be when she knew all was over. Her hands were closed very tight.

15th APRIL – Sister Butler found at Moutaza, brought to 17th at Victoria, buried at Chatby at 4pm. She was Sister in Charge at New Victoria Hotel.

16th APRIL – Calmer weather, also warmer.

17th APRIL – Miss Wilson left the Khedivial Hotel, went as Matron on 'Grantully Castle'. Miss J.Murphy took over the K.H. as Temporary Matron.

18th APRIL – Had a letter from Howard saying he had recd the £80 & put it in his bank till next war loan came on.

20th APRIL – (or thereabouts) sent £20 more to Howard to make up the £100.

26th APRIL – Easter Sunday – had an early service in the hotel, went to church in the evening. Jewish Passover completed (Sat).

27th APRIL – The great festival of the Arabs (the Sham-el-Nessim, breath of spring) when they turn out early morning, hug the grass & nature, everyone who can, goes into the country to hug nature. This happened to be the Greek festival (Easter), the end of the Passover, the Sham-el-Nessim & our Easter. Also on the 26th – Shakespeare's birthday. Heard of the air raid & bombs on Port Said, 2 companies of Worcesters, cut up near Mt Sinai by the Turks & General J.Wiggin killed. The Turks bringing up 2 mounted guns, mowed down the horses of our men, they were surrounded.

MAY – Gen. Townsend surrendered at Kut.

15th MAY – Miss Murphy left, with 71 Sisters, the 32 Gen. Hosp. Miss Beatrice Jones Q.S. Principal Matron for India accompanied them on the H.S. 'Dongola' Miss Mitchell A.E.(T.F.) Asst. Matron.

16th MAY – Appointed Matron of the Khedivial Hotel (nursing qrs).

21st MAY – Heard that the 23rd G.H. are at Amara. When we heard previously they were at Basra.

23rd MAY – The 33rd Gen Hosp. left us for Mesopotamia. Miss Orr being in charge, Miss Clayton-Smith Asst.

28th MAY – 22nd Stationary Hosp. left us (27 in all) Miss Macfarlane in charge. Temp. 101° – made arrangements for receiving 80 more Sisters, then went to bed – ordered there by Miss Oram.

29th MAY – 80 Sisters came, the 34th Gen Hosp. for Bombay, Miss Earle T.F. in charge.

30th MAY – Started packing, but only able to do a little, recd orders to go on *H.S. 'Dover Castle'* on the 1st June.

31st MAY – Finished packing when in my dressing gown, a deputation of Sisters came to my room bringing me an address, pair of field glasses, gong & cleopatra's needle. I was very pleasantly surprised.

1st JUNE – I went as Matron on the *H.M.H.S. 'Dover Castle'*. We looked round this ship, I was introduced to Major (…?…).

2nd JUNE – We took on 359 patients (34 sick Officers, 3 W. Officers) among these were 32 mental cases men & 2 mental Officers. We also had all the M.O.s & Orderlies of the No.1 Stat Hosp. N.Z.A.M.C.

6th JUNE – Passed Malta & recd the sad news of Lord Kitchener's death, by wireless, which cast a deep gloom on all.

8th JUNE – Picked up a Naval Surgeon, a Sister going on leave & a Corporal – we did not go in harbour. The sad news was confirmed & mourning ordered for a week.

9th JUNE – Passed close to the Portuguese coast.

10th JUNE – Passed Cape Finisterre at 1.50 keeping close in to the coast.

12th JUNE – Arrived Southampton, a bitterly cold day, disembarked patients soon after arrival at 6pm, were told we could not disembark as we must sail for Havre early next day.

13th JUNE – Left S'hampton at 7am, arrived Havre at 5pm. Miss Barton, A/Matron, came on board & we arranged to go to see three hospitals next day, 1 at the schools, the Casino & one previously an hotel. I went to see the hospital on the dock (the Station) which held 600 pts, they had many operations, about 10 or 11.

14th JUNE – Took 200 pts on, then went on a drive round Havre with Miss Barton visiting the various hospitals with her in Havre & Truville, which is very pretty. The rest of the patients, 345, came on in the afternoon & we left Havre about 5.40pm, arriving early next morning at S'hampton.

15th JUNE – We disembarked the patients before lunch & left that evening ourselves, going up to London for the night. I took the New Zealand Sisters for a bus ride & walk across the gardens & park (Hyde Park).

16th JUNE – Visited Sales my friends, & did a little shopping. I left by the 2.35 train for B'ham, Joe & John meeting me at the station. I left for Sutton Coldfield 4.45 but on arrival had to wait about 30 minutes for a cab. Found father looking very pleased, but older. My old school chum was there & while having tea Sis & Howard drove up in the motor.

17th JUNE – We went for a drive of 75 miles in the motor, having lunch at a pretty little place, Horecross, where is a beautiful church built by order of Lady Meynell-Ingram in memory of her husband. We arrived home in time for tea.

18th JUNE – Joe, Louie & Sam came.

19th JUNE – Monday – met Sis & Kath, went shopping, met Howard at lunch, after went to pictures & finished shopping, went to Nellies to tea. Dr Coule-Kneale coming to dinner.

20th JUNE – In morning called in town for things ordered & retd home at 3.30pm Mr Rudd came to tea.

21st JUNE – Father & I met Ada & Louie at Yardley, motored to Foleshill to Randles, then to Coventry for lunch, after which we drove over to Jack's at Pleasance Farm, Kenilworth.

Went into the woods, retd for tea, leaving for home at 7 o/c, we arrived 10 o/c after a very pleasant day. Found my wire telling me the boat *'Dover Castle'* sailed on Sat so had to return previous day.

22nd JUNE – Thursday – Went to town in the morning, friends came in evening, packed.

23rd JUNE – Friday – Left home 7.15am, arr London am. saw Edith Sale & left London 12.30pm arr S'hampton 2.10.

24th JUNE – Saturday – Went to paymaster & got the exes paid & rec'd pay books. Left S'hampton about 3.20pm.

25th JUNE – Sunday – Bit of a swell on. Had the —— 38th Gen Hosp. on board, Officers & men for Serbia (the 5th Hosp. to go there).

26th JUNE – Monday – Smooth sea but air damp.

4th JULY – Tuesday/ Wednesday – Arrived Salonika which looked very pretty from the sea. The Greek Islands we had passed were mostly very steep, many cultivated in parts & some cattle. As we arrived at Salonika the Mount Olympus stood boldly out on our left. The heat in this place was terrific, humid. We took the 38th Gen Hosp. Officers & men & hosp equipment. They were lent to the Serbian Gov't. They remained with us till the 9th then left us for their camp, on the side of the hill to the right of us beyond the Canadian hosp 45th & 50th, our 28th & 29th & 1st Canadians were on our left. Salonika is a very interesting place, but unpleasant as regards odours & pavements, re the roads having very worn cobbles.

5th & 6th JULY – We went on shore on Wednesday & Thursday. There were many French & Serbian soldiers as well as our own. The Serbs are very fine men. While resting under the shade of some trees, we met the Senior Chaplain Col. Dowding, who has been in Newcastle, S.A. He invited us in his cool room near. He was to come to lunch with us, but had an accident getting off the tram & could not come. We went to see the old church of St. George's which was about

2,000 yrs old. This was built by the Greeks, the roof is dome shaped, the body octagonal & there are 8 chapels in it. The roof is a fine piece of mosaic work. It was Greek for over 1,000 yrs then became a Turkish Mosque for over 500 yrs & since 1912 has been Greek. St Demetrious was the next church visited, also very, very old with two huge galleries running along the N.S & West ends, a very lofty church in fine Grecian style. The old city still has its walls running round but its suburbs seem to have spread in, which are some fine houses & a few pretty gardens. We did not get to the outskirts, where we hear grain & vegetables are growing. The bazaars were rather interesting to see, yet there was little of interest to buy. We got a cow bell. Some of the houses in the outer parts are built out, as in Cairo & their windows are of same style, only not so artistic. The 'Grantully Castle' was in dock, so Miss Wilson & some of her staff came on to tea with us.

8th JULY – We Sisters with the Major (Woollett) were invited to dinner to the A.S.C. mess belonging to the Serbian mission. We passed pleasant evening with them & watched two of the aviators mount, fly & dismount for our benefit & longed to go up. (We had been for a round of the outer bay in the motor launch).

9th JULY – 38th G.H. disembarked.

10th JULY – We moved into the inner harbour & took on patients.

11th & 12th JULY – Took on more patients, left on the 12th for Malta with 705 patients.

13th JULY – Our R.C. Chaplain Wai had a stroke.

14th JULY – Weather fairly good, but sea very unpleasant in its motion, making the Sisters rather ill.

15th JULY – Sea calm, pleasant breeze, patients better, including Padre & Sister Soirie.

16th JULY – Arrived at Malta on Sunday, started to disembark at 5pm. Lord Methuen & Gen Yeo came on in the afternoon, the former told the Major he remembered me. He shook hands, asked me if we had brought many patients & if they were very ill. They were a sad lot. Next day we went ashore for a short time as we left again at 12 noon. The journey back was very pleasant, except on the turning round into the Adriatic Sea. (took 2 new Sisters on).

17th JULY – Left Malta.

18th JULY – We passed what appeared in the distance ships, boats, looked through our glasses & could count 5. The Captain turned round, went to them, put off a boat with the chief Mr Linklala & 6 men, a destroyer came up after & said there had been a wreck, but the survivors had all been picked up earlier that morning. We passed boats, rafts, drawers, pieces of furniture, lifebelts, grain & all sorts of wreckage. The boats were named – she was the 'Ville de Rouen' of Havre, carrying our home mails to us. We prepared our two large upper wards for the survivors, thinking they might be wanted, as we counted 11 ship's boats. It was very sad & one wondered how many survivors there were & how many lost. We were forbidden to say anything by mouth at Sal. or by letter. They did not want it known. This delayed us some hours, so that instead of getting in Wed. evening we did not get in till Thursday morning.

20th JULY – Recd a letter from England & a paper. Embarked patients same morning & again in the evening.

21st JULY – Embarked patients making 686 in all – left at 4 o/c. It was a lovely sunset over Olympus. The Malea island where the —
    hermit & just above his little ——
    stone hut a chapel close —
    wards the sea with the —
    towering up above, the —
goats about & a few patches of apparently cultivated grounds but we could not tell what was growing. Each time one sees these islands, they seem to wear different aspects. We were much nearer to the shore than usual.
    (Troops from Egypt were disembarking 5,000 in all I heard).

22nd JULY – A very trying sea. All the Sisters were ill but one & myself & I did not feel at all comfortable. Fortunately our patients were not so ill as the former lot.

23rd JULY – Everyone looking seedy after yesterday's experience, sea calm, but weather hot & close.
(N.B. – Text and ——— indicates torn pages)

24th JULY – Arrived in Malta 2pm disembarked by 6pm. The Padre & Sister Sorrie whom we had left on our previous journey at Malta were, both improving, but neither fit for duty. Went on shore did a little shopping, after 1st visiting the B.R.C.S. Stores & given my order Col Lefeure staying late to take them. He informed us a piano was waiting for us, as we had requisitioned one before. We got it next day. Lord Methuen —

—— board directly we pulled

——– de the wharf & wanted

—— on the morrow, but he was informed, we must coal, so we were given another day.

25th JULY – Went to see Miss Acton who was A/Prin Matron – Miss Hoadley being away on holiday – heard Miss Sorrie my Sister I left behind on our previous visit was getting better. Asked how Sister Bickham & Hughes were getting on (they were the two T.F.Sisters I had taken on my staff from Malta 17/9/16) Sister Foster had been ill with slight gastro enteritis since the 21st & so we were still 2 short. Did a lot of shopping for one or another, retd to lunch, went ashore in the evening to see Sr Sorrie & met Mr Doherty & Captn Lawlers. Went with them to do a little shopping. We then went to the gardens by the lift & sat to see the view over the harbours & get the breeze till time to return to the boat for dinner. The view from above the saluting battery is very fine. I received 21 letters & 3 papers, so was busy in the afternoon. It was fine getting such a mail. These were old ones but interesting—
welcome. (the mail came on —

26th JULY – when we left Malta —   pm Had our piano from —
Rather a close day——

27th JULY – Busy with my —
X stores & looking —
Much more breezes —

28th JULY – Passed Cape Matapan & Cape Malea – this latter is where the hermit lives on the lower part of a very steep rocky cliff. At 8am we passed the 'La France' Hosp. Ship. She was a very large 4 funnel steamer double decker.

29th JULY – Arrived Salonika at 9.30am the 'Letitia' in, she finished loading & was off in the afternoon. Our patients began to come at 6.30pm finished at 10 o/c

(687 in all) this making 2,078 we had taken on our boat since 10th July. We were told to go next morning, (thunder storms).

30th JULY – Left Salonika for Malta at 2pm. Mostly malaria cases, a few dysentery & enterics & one or two surgical (ord). Only 3 Officers (pts) Col Ferguson D.D.M.S. lines of communication. Major Scott, Lt Mudie. The B.R.C.S. Commissioner came on board – Col Courthall – Thompson. He is going to Malta & after to Italy. He is the Commissioner for Mediterranean Forces B.R.C.S. Egypt etc. French troop ship brought in a
—— number of Russian troops &
—— ending them in the afternoon
—— a service in the evening
——— well attended (voluntary)
——— phones are being well used
——— appreciated.
  The lightening was lovely sheet & forked together for some hours & heavy rains.

31st JULY – The islands have looked lovely today. We left the Dore Gulf & island at 10.30am. The island of Euboea looked fine, the clouds were so lovely & the lights & shades added to the beauty. There is a good size town on the island & some villages. I believe the port is on the other side. Grain, currants, grapes, melons & other fruits are grown on this the largest of these Greek Islands. We passed about noon, another transporter (French) with Russian troops to Salonika & a French Hosp. Ship the 'Sphinx'. A good sized British Air Ship went out with us yesterday & was with us for several hours & waved to us.

1st AUGUST – Had a close night – little air, making us feel as if we had not any energy left in us. We passed Matapan about 7.45pm in previous evening. Had a good concert for the men.

2nd AUGUST – Arrived Malta 2pm discharged pts 687 at 4.30pm.

3rd AUGUST – Went to Citta Veechia in the Cathedral, St Pauls Grotto & the Catacombs. The former was a very fine building made ———
of some of the pillars, were ———
the floor was beautiful, ——
bishops & knights of St John ———

buried there. The gilt——

but somehow there——

appearance above——

The grotto where St Paul lived for three months had a very fine statue (marble) of him. The catacombs extend for 7 miles, very rough, all of them not high. Saw some lace workers there in the old town. Lord Methuen gave an address to a great crowd to the principal square.

St. Paul's Cathedral, Rabat – circa 2002.

St. Paul's Cathedral
Grotto – circa 2002.

4th AUGUST – Service in the cathedral of St Peter, C of E Festival of St Domenico, processions in the town.

5th AUGUST – Embarked 603 pts & 41 Officers, including Sister Sorrie & Mrs Wilkinson, who was a mental pt (Officer's wife).

6th AUGUST – Passed 3 torpedo destroyers, a service 7 & 10.30.

7th AUGUST – Sister Sorrie X rayed (nothing abnormal to be seen). Lunch time – a troop ship crossed our stern flying the Italian flag & kept with us nearly touching us at times. A concert this evening to the men, fearfully sultry day.

8th AUGUST – A whale was seen

—— in 50 yds of our starboard side

——arrived Gibraltar at 6.30

——— at 7.15 (just to receive orders

————sea a little choppy.

————am one of the patients

———— he died the previous night.

11th AUGUST – Passed Cape Finisterre very early in the morning, boat rolling well, saw some whales, one very close to the port side.

13th AUGUST – Arrived at Southampton. Disembarked patients in the evening.

14th AUGUST – Went at 7am up to the Brambles off Netley Hosp. S.O.S. for France.

15th AUGUST – Went into dry dock, left for home by 3pm. Train arrived home at 10pm, found father fairly well.

21st AUGUST – Retd to the boat much better for the rest & cooler weather.

22nd AUGUST – Left dock at 11am for the Brambles once more.

Katy wrote a letter home as follows:

H.M.H.S. Dover Castle
S'hampton

Dear Sis

We are still here as you see by the address. I think we are going east on Sunday, loading up Saturday, but to what part I know not. We expected to be sent to Havre & so have got one trip in in the time, but other ships came in & so we are here still. I have been on shore to get expenses paid up & the pay books. Our boat's company, the union castle line send a launch out in the morning & afternoon, as otherwise we could not communicate with the shore, we are out in the Brambles again. It is very pretty on either side of us & we long to explore, but there is plenty of work to be done, to get ready the wards, cannot explain. While on shore this morning, I was greeted by the Matron of the 'H.M.H.S Salta' & informed that she was carrying your parcel (to me) about with her till today, when as it seemed very unlikely they would be going East, she thought it best to hand it over to Cox's shipping Co. I went with her & recovered it, fortunately. Everything was in splendid order & the chocolates. I thank you, also for

the collar. Fancy getting it here. It would probably been ages longer, before
I received it, if ever. I was fortunate in meeting Miss Harries, she is on the
Harve run. They take the patients (in alternate loads) to Dublin. I hope
you will all have a jolly time at Newquay. Miss Hayne, Mrs Hynes (Miss
Shepherd, when you saw her), & Dolly Sale met me at Euston. Everyone
thinks I look much better for my few days. Much love to you all
    From your loving sister Katy.

23rd AUGUST – Went on shore, saw Miss Harries, Matron of the 'Salta', who had a parcel for me, one I thought had gone astray.

26th AUGUST – Went in dock again at 9am. In the afternoon went to the Dock Red X stores & then in town for tea. After tea 5 of us went for a ride to Hampton Park, then to the river Itchin, which was very pretty, we went some distance along the banks, returned to the docks for dinner & afterwards to the theatre.

27th AUGUST – Took on 6 R.A.M.C ———
& men & 42 C.R.A.M.C. non ——
1 naval surgeon, 1 Q 2 M.a———
1 R.A.M.C., Cptn, W.I.Regt & ———
W.I. Regt a new M.O.———
Joined us in place of ———
Had completed his time. Left the same day.

28th & 29th AUGUST – Rough sea, many feeling ill, none too grand myself, uncomfortable & headache.

30th AUGUST – Lovely day, so fresh & bright. Everyone feeling better.

31st AUGUST – Arrived at Gibraltar where the W.Indians have to transfer to the 'Magdelena', not yet arrived. Very cold wind coming through the Straits. Sir Brigham sprained his ankle.

1st SEPTEMBER – 'Magdelena' in early this morning, but has to land her gun & coal. Colonel Lewis invited Major Woollett to lunch but none of us able to go ashore. Harbour is very busy.

2nd SEPTEMBER – Lovely morning. W.I pts still with us.

3rd SEPTEMBER – *'Magdelena'* came alongside, after discharging her gun. The patients were transferred about 12 noon. We left about 1pm. The *'Magdelena'* left directly after.

5th SEPTEMBER – Strong wind sprang up in the night, but all was quiet before breakfast.

7th SEPTEMBER – Arrived at Malta 9.30am – (a large steamer sunk off Malta (Gozo) the submarine was caught) pleasant weather. Went on shore
—— 11am & again in the evening to
———enquiries about a friend in hosp
——— he left for England on the 22nd
——— Malta, saw one of our
——— marines soon after we left, & many trawlers. Sister Mullers & Sister Collyer joined.

9th SEPTEMBER – Passed some wreckage in the evening – what was apparently a sideboard, a life belt box, a stool & a life belt, but no name to be seen on the latter. In the morning a vessel wired that she was being chased, message came twice & then later that she had got away. We saw several lots of mine sweepers in threes.

10th SEPTEMBER – A beautiful day, sky, sea & islands were fine. Went to early service which was well attended.

11th SEPTEMBER – Arrived at Salonika.

12th SEPTEMBER – Went on shore in the morning & to the old tower. Patients embarked 104 in the evening.

13th SEPTEMBER – 80 patients embarked in the morning & more in the evening.

14th SEPTEMBER – More patients.

15th SEPTEMBER – Left Salonika at 11am.

18th SEPTEMBER – Arrived in Malta, disembarked our patients, 213 cot, the others walking cases (568 total).

19th SEPTEMBER – Saw Miss Beedon-Smith the principal Matron, went to lunch with
     Miss Acton (T.F. Matron) at (…?…)
     From which there is a grand view
     We left about 10am next day.

20th SEPTEMBER – Left Malta.

21st SEPTEMBER – Rather rough.

22nd SEPTEMBER – Very hot still……
Night a strong …….
Sprang up about midnight.

23rd SEPTEMBER – Arrived at Salonika, the 6th hospital boat in harbour. Still a piercing cold wind.

24th SEPTEMBER – Went to see Miss Wilson, the Principal Matron at the 5th Can. Hosp.

25th SEPTEMBER – Colonel Sutton D.D.M.S. made arrangements for me to see my friend Miss M. E. Thomson at the 27th Clearing Station, Lahana close to the Struma Valley. I had permission to take two friends, so Rev M. Warner & Sister Bilton accompanied me. We were informed that all was arranged for us, a special boat (naval) called for us at the '*Dover Castle*' at 6.10pm which took us to the marble steps, we then proceeded to the D.D.M.S. Office where a car was waiting to take us to the 5th Can. Hosp. where we were received by Miss Wilson (the Matron). We all had dinner together then the padre was taken to the Officers Mess & we were shown to our tent (sick sisters, empty) we were much amused by our surroundings & the incidents of the evening.

26th SEPTEMBER – We were called at 5.45 breakfasted at 6.30am at the
……office the padre joined us
……about 7.45am in an
…….opened), going up with the
……..bring patients to the base
     We went to Lahana 56 kilometres up country. Every bit of the way was very interesting, showing something of the huge work on hand in providing for the

troops & all things requisite to carry on the war & preparations to protect the road. Besides these camps or dumps as they are called are various large & small hospitals. The country is very pretty, range after range of hills & the valleys & gorges are very pretty. There were interesting groups of men, Turks as well as Greeks & Serbians making the road wider & repairing. Here & there quaint villages on the sides of the hills. The earth looks rather like that of Devonshire, red fields were being ploughed. Grapes, melons, pears, damsons were to be bought from the villagers – vegetable marrows, potatoes & tomatoes. The natives were preparing their Indian corn for grinding. We arrived at Lahana about 12.15pm having gone 7½ kilometres too far, the driver lost his way. We were at the end

Of the Struma Valley on that side….

Huge hills on either side so we……

To ask the way to the 27th C.C.S…..

Miss Thomson was delighted…..

& made us very welcome…….

Lunch, then the padre……

To Padre Phillips C of E…...

I went to rest a while.

Went to see the Hosp. with Sister Falkner (N.Z.ans) whom she met in London. We were very surprised to see such a lovely spread at tea time. The hosp cook having made & sent over for us very good cakes & tarts. The hosp is prettily situated on the side of a famous & historical hill in the last Balkan war. It lies near the Struma, one range of hills lying between them. From the top of this hill could be seen another part of the valley (Struma). Trenches were being dug (some were finished) & dug outs made. Wire entanglements were about the top of the hill. The hosp contained 250 beds, but they nearly always had 250 stretchers in tents full of pts. They had 30 in one tent. The patients were brought down from the front all day either on mule stretchers or small horse ambulances, the tops of which were splashed with dabs of paint of different shades. Every morning 20 ambulances left the C.C.S with pts for the base & retd same evening.

……sometimes another lot of 20 left at

…….as well. In the surgical wards

…….- ter number of cases at this time

…….- ther abdominal or chest cases.

……wounds, arm & leg

……week an aerial bomb

had been dropped on some out places near the hosp, but the bomb did not explode. An apology was sent by the young German airman later when he knew it was a hospital. In the evening Miss Thomson accompanied us to the village where Padre Phillips seemed to have made acquaintance with all the inhabitants, receiving smiles from nearly all the women & children & shaking hands with all the men. We were seeking to buy eggs & eventually succeeded in buying 6 at *[handwritten: 2½ each.]*

It was so interesting entering the courtyards of these people. The houses are 2 story high, the top which is the living part is entered by outside wooden steps running up to a covered wooden veranda. The lower one seems to be used for stores or stables. They are built of rough stone with cement thrown in between the stones. Several families live in one house (relations, evidently). Some of the Greek women were very pretty & the men were rather good looking, not large men. The inhabitants were mostly Turks, but the women ran away when we tried to get near them. There was a quaint Greek Church, like an old barn with a cross painted on the door. There was also a small mosque in the village. We returned to dinner. The padre going to the Officers mess. They came up to ours after dinner, Mr Butler (Lt.Q.) whom we brought out from England was attached to the mess. He said he could give us a run in his car as he was going up on business, but we were afraid as we expected to receive word we were to go early next day. I shared Miss Thomson's tent. It was cold in the night.

27th SEPTEMBER – Arose at 7.30am & had brkft at 8. After which we went up to the hospital. About 9am we went up the historical hill & got a good view of the Struma. We found some cyclamen growing & some very pretty wild flowers. I found a very pretty blue orchid near the stream, towards the foot of the hill, similar to a bee orchid, but unfortunately I lost it on the way back to the boat. As we were nearing the foot of the hill, we heard firing in the air & saw a Bulgar aeroplane racing toward the hospital, the firing still continuing about 1 mile away, we lay down gazing at the little white puffs of cloud made by the firing & I saw distinctly a little black spec, immediately another shot just in front of it caused it to go up higher & I saw the last shot (we heard the firing of the big guns in the valley in the previous evening & several times in the morning) which from where we were lying seemed to be within a foot of it. After that we did not see it at all. It did not drop, so I think both got away. We all – Mr Warner & Mr Phillips, Sister Bilton & I then went to the village & had an interesting walk. We returned by 11.30, had some tea & biscuits & left by the 12 o/c convoy. We headed the convoy which had to be stopped several times for the pts benefit, one man having a rigor, at one stop. We had a dusty, but an enjoyable ride, arrived at the ferry by 4.50pm in a very dusty condition. Felt all the better after a bath & tea. We had all thoroughly enjoyed the trip. I found patients had arrived, so went round to see them. Several wounded officers from the Dorian side of the Struma, sick & wounded men from there & from the Seres side.

28th SEPTEMBER – Took on more patients making total 565 (White R.A.M.C.T ord. put in padded cell).

29th SEPTEMBER – Left Sala at 9.30am patients – mostly cot cases looking very weak.

30th SEPTEMBER – Patients on the whole a little better, one in 7 [ward] worse.

1st OCTOBER – Sea rather rough, all patients slightly better.

2nd OCTOBER – Arrived at Malta 9 o/c went into Marsa Sirocco Bay, to await orders. Orders to go to Hamilton Wharf, Valletta, came at 10 o/c arrived there about 12.45, disembarked pts about 4.30. Went to see Miss Beedsmore-Smith & to the Red X & ordered things for M.E.Thomson.

3rd OCTOBER – Left Malta at 4 o/c.

4th OCTOBER – Wireless signal recd from 'Franconia' who signalled SOS at 10.30am erratic course signalled * Latitude 35° 56N. Long 18° 30E*. 10.50am recd another signal from 'Franconia' "Am sinking" 'Dover Castle' 28½ miles distant altered course. Speed 16.4 knots. First sited wreckage at 11.30am then 14 miles distant. When we first sighted her she was listing to starboard, she gave a twist round, stern came out of the water shortly after, when she dived quietly down. I did not see her after she turned round & I went down to order things for the survivors. All beds & hot water bottles were ready. Beef tea & coffee ready. We arrived on the scene of disaster at 12.35pm. 15 boats came in. 12 men were lost. The torpedo struck her amidships, very soon after the platforms in engine room were below water. Two men were injured one, McDonald a stoker badly scalded was very ill the 1st 2 days. (302 of the Officers & crew & 6 passengers). All came on board so orderly without any confusion. Captn Miller the Com. & Dr McKenzie (the ship's Dr) coming on from nearly the last boat. We resumed our course at 1.10pm taking the rescued crew to Sala with us. Officers & men were very grateful for everything done for them. We tried to clothe them all so as to be warm from the ordnance & Red X store.

5th OCTOBER – Had a very busy day with the rescued. Patients a little better.

6th OCTOBER – Arrived Salonica.

7th OCTOBER – Capt'n Miller, Officers & crew left us about 10am very full of gratefulness & when on the barge, gave out ringing cheers for us all. All the R.A.M.C. staff & crew came up to give them hearty cheers & God speed. Many ships in the harbour wondering why all this shouting should be as the news was not known, except to the very few either on sea or land. We took patients on the same evening 161.

8th OCTOBER – More patients embarked making the total 596. This with our own sick making 601.

9th OCTOBER – Left at 6am orders are to go only 10 knots in the hr. About 2/3 of the patients are wounded from the Struma Valley (from all parts of it).

10th OCTOBER – After dinner about 8pm we noticed a peculiar light on our port side some distance ahead. As we neared her there was a distinct smell of oil or paraffin. The light was white & flashing we passed turned & went round the light which was from a life belt another light appeared ahead & then came a red light, as we neared this the smell of paraffin was very strong. As we came nearer we could see distinctly 4 boats, only one with a light. It came up to us, as we stopped a few yds away. The Captain & 4 Officers with 6 of the crew came on board up the rope ladder thrown out for them. They were from the 'Etac' of the Sheer Line (paraffin boat). The submarine fired many shells into her before she sank. They attacked her about 3pm. She did not sink till after 6.30pm. A Wilson Liner, although warned, picked up the rest of the crew, the Captn etc staying by to see the ships sink. The liner had to go off quickly as the submarine came up & chased her. She the 'Etac' had been escorted till (she reached the danger zone) about 4 or 5 hrs before she was attacked. The crew were Chinese.

11th OCTOBER – Received wireless of 5 submarines having been seen in a few hours near to us. Very smooth glassy like sea.

12th OCTOBER – Arrived Marsa Sirocco Bay at about 6.30am (Capt'n Watchlin of 'H.M.S Jonquil' came on board & had a chat). Left for Malta about 10 o/c, 9 submarines were reported between Matapan & N. of Malta. Arrived at

Hamilton Wharf about 1.45pm. Disembarked early evening. Sister Bilton taken ill in the night.

13th OCTOBER – Went on shore shopping in the morning, had lunch with Miss Beedsmore-Smith at her flat. 5 ships reported sunk by submarines, two in St Paul's Bay. Crews were rescued & one small transport was rowed into the grand harbour Valletta. The 'H.M.T. Tunisian' was in harbour. Captn Gillies came on board.

14th OCTOBER – 'H.M.T. Tunisian' filling with troops for Salonica (Mother's birthday). Saw the torpedo destroyer 88 which caught the submarine who sank the 'H.M.T Franconia' & spoke to us when picked up the crew. We left Malta at 10.45am. A beautifully calm sea.

15th OCTOBER – Calm sea, rather warm air. Passed Matapan about 9.30pm.

16th OCTOBER – Delightful air & the sea beautiful, the whole aspect fine. We noticed, just as we entered the gulf of (…?…) there was quite a large camp on Uboea Island, which was not there when we passed previously. It seemed to us to be the result of 'M.t. Veneznelos' visit & that they were the revolutionists tents.

17th OCTOBER – Arrived at 7o/c (am) at Salonica. One of the Greek torpedo destroyers in harbour 'Venezuelos' is here, 'Landovery Castle', 'Guildford', 'Herefordshire', 'Valdivia', 'Warilda' & 'Wandilla' in harbour. In the evening the 'Guildford' went out & the 'Esequibo' took her place.

18th OCTOBER – The 'Valdivia' (had taken pts on at Stavos Bay) filled up & went out, so did the 'Warilda'. 'Tunisian' arrived.

19th OCTOBER – Lovely day, went on shore saw many of the Italian troops march, thro the town in their grey uniforms & steel helmets. In 3 days 11,000 troops, Italian, had arrived at Salonica, the 'Tunisian' brought from Malta 2,300 British soldiers.

20th OCTOBER – Two French, two Italian & one British troop ships arrived in harbour, the French & Italian seem wisely to send their ships in couples. Two empty ones left in the evening. The 'Tunisian' & the 'Lord Nelson' left about 4.30pm escorted by one of our destroyers.

21st OCTOBER – A French gun boat left, escort (Trafalgar day).

26th OCTOBER – Took on 151 pts.

27th OCTOBER – Took on more pts making a total of 608 & 2 passengers. A Pres. Minister Cumpton & a Canadian Sister Mrs Guilbride of the 5th Can. Gen. Sal. who is proceeding home on leave.

28th OCTOBER – Left Salonica 2.30pm rather cold wind blowing.

29th OCTOBER – Still a cold wind blowing.

30th OCTOBER – Lovely day. At 12.45pm I saw a submarine (re the submarine seen so long) about 1½ miles from our port side (not escorted), she remained in sight till 1pm when we went to lunch. After dinner the Chief & 2 M.O's corroborated the fact of the German submarine, one of the latest type.

31st OCTOBER – Arrived in Malta at 12.50pm discharged pts 608 & passengers 2.

1st NOVEMBER – Recd invitation from Lady Methuen to go to tea. I went & had a very pleasant time with her ladyship & Miss Phipps (her niece) at the old Palace San Antonia.

2nd NOVEMBER – Padre Warner left us at 9am to embark on the 'Osouza' (P.O.boat) used as a naval messenger to go to Italy Larons, through Italy & France & so home as his contract would end Nov 4th. Mr Cumpton Pres. Padre, whose contract had expired went with him. The boat left at 10.30am, Lady Methuen & her niece came to see the ship at 11.45 & seemed very interested. An invitation had come for the whole staff to visit them at San Antonio Palace that afternoon, she expressed a wish I would come again with the Sisters, so I went.

We met Lt Gordon-Mitchell A.D.C. to his Lordship, & the Officers off the 'Caledonian' who were on the way to Salonika & are to transfer to the 'H.T.Tunisian' on Tuesday following

San Antonio Palace.

3rd NOVEMBER – Went ashore in the morning. Called to see Sr Bilton who was admitted to hospital for Sisters on the 31 /10/ 16. She was rather better.

4th NOVEMBER – Left Malta at 3pm for Salonika, 10 Sisters & 1 nurse came on for duty in Sal. They are returning after sick leave.

5th NOVEMBER – Recd S.O.S. signal early this morning, 2nd recd "'Valdivia' picked up the 2 crews" Passed 4 boats of a wreck at 7.30am (the ships wrecked were 2 small ones).

7th NOVEMBER – Arrived at Salonica, 7 other boats (Hosp) in, but only 4 of ours.

8th NOVEMBER – Went ashore. It is the 4th Anniversary of the Greek Capture of Salonica. An official Thanksgiving service was held in St Demetrius Church. We saw the procession of Venizelos, his parliament & Army Corps with 2 bands, pass to & from the church. The men wore khaki serge, gray field caps. The Greek Admiral (…?…) & other naval officers also were in the procession.

10th NOVEMBER – Captn Flewitt who is stationed at the 41st Gen Hosp. (Serbian) came on board to see me & stayed to lunch.

11th NOVEMBER – It is reported that the Austrians have given the order to evacuate Trieste. British & French war boats are flying the Italian flag (apparently in honour of this).

12th NOVEMBER – Left Salonica at 7.20am sea very smooth. After leaving the harbour we saw about 40 mine sweepers at work, laying the nets for a submarine which had gone towards Salonica. There were also 2 destroyers at work. About 4pm a strong wind got up & the sea got quite choppy.

13th NOVEMBER – Recd a wireless from Malta via destroyer to "proceed to Alexandria & discharge the patients", so had to alter our course. We passed Crete during the night.

14th NOVEMBER –Had an afternoon concert for the patients on the well deck.

15th NOVEMBER – Arrived at Alex at 9.30am discharged pts same morning. Miss Oram came on about 11.25am, went to her office at 3.30 & again after tea.

Saw Mrs Richmond & Captn Richmond. All my Sisters except 2 to leave me, 6 months up.

16th NOVEMBER – The Sisters left in the afternoon. I had a very busy day, with receiving stores, arranging about giving in disp. stores, filling in all sorts of forms & confidential reports, kept busy till after 5pm, when I dressed & went to the office. Went to Dartons to supper, found Joey had retd from England. Mrs Stephenson there, she had lost her baby boy 12 days before, he was born in August. Retd to boat at 9pm.

17th NOVEMBER – Miss Oram came about 11.50am & took Sis Mullen, Colyer & myself back in her motor at 12.15pm sent us to the pay office. The 2 Sisters returning to lunch & I called again to see the 4 Sisters from Ras-el-Tin at the pay office at 3pm their pay was settled. I had had a busy morning receiving the 7 new Sisters taking their particulars, making out the new plans for the wards, installing the Sisters, taking them round & explaining all to them, then reading the rules & talking to them. I left them orders what to do. Sister Mullen was placed in charge to go round twice to see all was going on with their work. The 4 Sisters returning to cut up dressings etc. The men had got on well with their ward considering the coaling was not finished till early morning. I returned about 6.45pm having gone to Ras-el-Tin to see Miss Bond & to explain about the pay books of 3 of my Sisters who had left the boat the previous day.

18th NOVEMBER – Received 525 pts & 14 Indian ord, the patients to transfer to the 'Britannic' for home at Mudros, the orderlies to go with us to Sal. for pts. Learn from Sis Collyer that Breedon K.D.O. has been put off.

19th NOVEMBER – Went to early service, our new C of E padre came on Friday 17th, Mr Wilcox from the 'Letitia'.

20th NOVEMBER – Arrived in Mudros at 6pm. The appearance is very different from that of last year. There are very few tents & a few huts. About 5 naval (war boats). The 'Landovery', 'Glenart Castle', 'Wandilla', 'Warilda', 'St Margaret', 'Herefordshire' (the latter came next day & ourselves) were all in the harbour waiting for the 'Britannic' to tranship our pts from Malta to Alex to her.

21st NOVEMBER – The 'Herefordshire' arrived about 11am with the news she had recd S.O.S. from the 'H.S. Britannic' that she had struck a mine or been torpedoed in the Kea channel off Port Nicolo. It was thought she could get in, but we heard later that she had sunk, the staff & crew picked up by mine sweeper & small transport. An enemy aeroplane came & was driven away by ours. We recd orders at 4am to proceed to Malta, so left at 5.30pm. A slight gale blowing.

22nd NOVEMBER – Passed the *'Herefordshire'* & *'Glenart'* Hospital Ships. We passed the islands of Anti-Milo & Milo (off the Asiatic Coast) in the afternoon about 2 – 2.30.

23rd NOVEMBER – Had wireless message, the Admiralty report that the *'Britannic'* sunk in the Aegean Sea, on the 21st inst. either mined or torpedoed. 1,106 survivors, of whom 282 are injured, a cruiser or destroyer was near, but too far off.

24th NOVEMBER – Arrived Malta, at Hamilton Wharf, at about 2 o/c, then told we were to take pts on to fill up our beds. We had from Alex 525, so took on 80, making total of 625 (65 Officers, 6 Wt off, 554 men). We were told that 2 submarines attacked the *'Britannic'*, one on either side, each putting 2 torpedoes in her. News also was given as to the *'Braemar Castle'* sunk in the Kea Channel in the morning. News came later that the Captn had managed to beach her & all were safe. The *'Valdivia'* was sent to take off the patients, staff & crew. She left that afternoon. We left at 4pm.

25th NOVEMBER – Had a rough night. Very rough sea, a dirty day. *'Landovery Castle'* which left a short time before us was in sight most of the day. The boat rolled tremendously & all day breakages everywhere were going on. We passed a large troop ship going the same way as we were, she seemed constantly to make for our bows, to be in a way at the mercy of the storm. We were glad when she got behind us. We passed two cargo boats & Cape Bond on our port side.

26th NOVEMBER – Had a rough night, still rather rough. Passed Milo & Anti-Milo on the port side. Saw *'Landovery Castle'*.

27th NOVEMBER – By wireless, heard that there was a furious cyclone off Sardinia, we got the end of it, quite bad enough & very many things smashed. Better still a calm day, but very cold.

28th NOVEMBER – Arrived at Gibraltar soon after 9am, cloudy. *'Landovery Castle'* came in shortly after, stopped to take a few patients on, we had not any spare beds. She was astern on our port side, till she passed us at midnight.

29th NOVEMBER – Bright sunshine, not quite so cold, but rather choppy.

30th NOVEMBER – On the outskirts of the bay of Biscay, a big roll owing to the swell.

1st DECEMBER – Lovely day but still big swell on.

2nd DECEMBER – Arrived S'hampton in the afternoon, disembarked patients, settled accounts with pay master.

3rd DECEMBER – 7am Put out, off Netley, very cold day. Orders for Havre.

4th DECEMBER – Left S'hampton 6am & off Harve 3.30 had to anchor till 7pm then went into the harbour. *'H.S. Galeka'* lying to the left. Took patients on 514 at 8.30, nearly all cot cases, then 20 at 11.45pm & 31 about 1am. Miss Blakely (Matron) came on board. We left Harve at 3.30am arrived S'hampton. Total no of pts 565. Total number of pts carried from 2/6/16 – 4/12/16 is 7, 951 + 806 RAMC Off + men & crew of wrecked vessels. Total carried 8, 757.

5th DECEMBER – Left Harve at 3.30am. Had a very good passage, arrived about 1.30pm. Disembarked pts at 22 Dock in the afternoon. Went to the Red X stores & found the bales sent from Sutton for me, cushions, bags etc. In the evening went with Mr Maitland, Mr Scott, Sister Collyer went to see 'Potash & Perlmutt'. It was very good. Captn Culverwell left.

6th DECEMBER – We left the harbour & lay off Cowes at 6am. Equipment of wards taken & handed over to Captn Pembertly as the O/C Major Woolett was leaving & he Pembertly was taking over.

7th DECEMBER – *'Aquitania'* came out & passed us. We (7 of us) went ashore to Cowes, crossed the ferry & went to Osborne House, saw the grounds & house, went into the dining room where Queen Victoria lay in state. At one end was the low table & chairs used by the young princes & princesses that of King Edward's having the Prince of Wales feathers on the back. The princes chairs had arms. We went to the drawing room & billiard room off it. The billiard table had not been used since Prince Consort died. We saw the outside of the room, with its large bay window where Queen Vic died. It was never open to any visitors. We went through the picture galleries, but the Durbar room was not open. We saw our new Captn in Cowes. He was just going on with the purser to take over command. Our chief Engineer was also leaving us for a time as his wife was very ill and was to have an operation. Yesterday it had been arranged that the chief was to take command and the others move up in consequence. Went we retd to the boat we found the O/C had had a letter and left us. He was to take charge of a train. At 8pm we started again for Harve.

8th DECEMBER – Arrived at Harve, went along side the quay about 10am. All the Sisters and myself went ashore in the afternoon (very showery weather). We heard in the morning that the *'Landovery Castle'* who had gone to take the prisoners (exchange ones) off the *'Dunluce Castle'* after she was badly damaged, was on fire and had had to put her passengers ashore at Dover.

9th DECEMBER – Lovely day. Took on 266 pts in the morning, expected the others in the afternoon, but they did not come till after 11pm. Took 347 making the total 613 including 68 Germans. Left at 12.10am had a good passage.

10th DECEMBER – Lovely bright day. Arrd S'hampton at 3pm. Disembarked pts, we were ready to leave, but could not as General Donovan was away for the weekend.

11th DECEMBER – Ordered a dress at Mayers & Co East St and was fitted. General did not come on till 5.30pm. We caught the 6.5 train up to London, stayed the night at Howard De Walden Club at 35 Langham St.

12th DECEMBER – Went home by the 1.20 from Euston arriving at 'South View' [family home, Sutton Coldfield] by 5pm.

13th DECEMBER – Stayed at home.

14th DECEMBER – Went to Joe and Louie's and to Salloways.

15th DECEMBER – Went to town met Howard, Sis, Ada, Kath & Dorrington.

16th DECEMBER – Went to Captn Flewitts, Mrs Flewitt not at home as Teddy the eldest was having an operation for (Appendix), doing well. Cycled home, changed into uniform to go to an amateur dramatic at the School of Art, B'ham, which Kath & her friend Miss Holcroft got up on behalf of the Lady Mayoress War fund. The play was 'Diedre' an old Irish play. Kath took the part of Fergus, Howard, Sam, Ada, Katy and Dor were present. It was well done. They were asked to do it for the same purpose in two other places. I went home with Howard. It was so foggy Sis did not go. I was 2¼ hrs in the train instead of ½ hr.

17th DECEMBER – Father's birthday. Howard drove me home in the motor. We called at Acocks Green for Joe who came to dinner, Sam also came. In the evening Mr H Ansell and Mr Lorrimer called about taking a parcel for Captn Flewitt.

18th DECEMBER – Left Sutton Coldfield 7.20am, B'ham at 8.40, arrd Euston 10.45. Dollie met me and went with me to W'loo where I booked my luggage and went to Beckenham to see Mr Warner. I had a very pleasant time with him and his sister whom I liked very much. Mrs Warner, his mother, was ill. Left at 6pm caught the 7pm from W'loo with Sister Collyer and Mr Wilcox, arrd at S'hampton at 10pm. Could not get a cab till a young naval officer kindly asked us to use his, so we all scrambled in, our luggage tied on here and there. He had to wait at the gates till the cab went back as he had not a pass.

20th DECEMBER – A quiet birthday, went shopping.

21st DECEMBER – Had fire drill at 2pm as a new order had been made out, each to our boats. Left S'hampton at 3pm. Saw the lights of Victoria and dimly the lights of the Needles about 9pm. Lieut Prince a new M.O.

22nd DECEMBER – A lovely sunny morning, warmer, sea rather choppy.

23rd DECEMBER – Very rough, not very cold in the sun, heavy showers.

24th DECEMBER – 6 at early service. The orderlies free till Tuesday. Smooth during the night, but by 8.30 very rough again, muggy weather. There was a united service in the evening held by Mr Wilcox (C of E), Keeler preached. Several Sisters went. Carols sung at 10pm by Sisters and orderlies.

25th DECEMBER – A lovely morning, but still rather rough. About 20 at early service, the Chaplain about 20 mins late. Service at 10.30am, orders were for everyone except Jews and R.C.'s to attend so every Officer was present except Captn Lauertine. In the afternoon the Sisters drew lots for their places at the 3 tables for dinner. Very pleasant dinner and a good concert given in the 7 ward at 9.30pm. Sea quite calm from about 4pm.

26th DECEMBER – Lovely bright morning, sea calm. We passed Gibraltar very early. Went down to Red X stores and commenced taking stock.

29th DECEMBER – Arrived Malta mid day, told we were to start at 4pm only had ¾ hr ashore, went to learn about Sis Bilton, found she had not recovered sufficiently for the boat and that it would not be wise to do boat duty again. Captn Remberthy apptd Major (recd wire).

30th DECEMBER – Did not get the stores disembarked soon enough to leave the previous day, so did not leave Malta till 10am today. We heard yesterday they (mine sweepers) picked up many mines off Malta & Marsa Scala Bay. We were told it was a good thing that we did not come the evening before.

31st DECEMBER – Bright day, but cooler.

1917

1st JANUARY – Had S.O.S. message from 'Ivernia' (Cunard boat) but we were over 200 miles from her. She was torpedoed in the (...?...) channel, had 2,000 troops (ours) on board, only 900 survivors.

2nd JANUARY – Arrived at Salonica, anchored about 10am. Seven Hosp. ships in harbour 'Gloucester', 'Grantullt', 'Letitia', 'Asturias', 'Herefordshire', 'Panama' and 'St Margaret of Scotland'. Took the Sisters ashore by the 1.20 ferry. We (3) went through the bazaar and up the hill beyond the walls. The other Sisters turned back. Heard the 'Letitia' on her return from Marseilles early part of Dec had picked up over 300 survivors from the 'City of B'ham', passenger ship, they were mostly women and children of our soldiers who had left India. Shortly after they had picked up a 2nd crew and passengers about 200 from the 'Carnac' and proceeded to Alexandria.

3rd JANUARY – Captn Flewitt came on board to lunch, he is still at the 41st Gen hosp. He took his parcels from home. He told us of an Irish woman who had been living out here who did not want to go home so joined as a Serb soldier and had become a staff sergeant. While lying wounded in hospital, one of the Serb Generals came and decorated her with the highest Serbian honour she could receive for bravery and conspicuous military service rendered. She was named Sands and came from Kerry. There was also a Serbian Sergeant (woman) who had been very brave and was brought in wounded for the 6th time, but would get better and hoped to go up again to the firing line. Not a nice woman, but very plucky and a good soldier. These were both in the 41st in December. We were informed that they had had air raids every day about 1pm, no damage done except by our own anti aircraft guns, but they had all been driven off, but one, which was hit in the petrol tank, so was brought down whole by the Italians' camp. No air ship had been seen by us on the 2nd or 3rd. Heard Miss Wilson is back at K. Hotel.

4th JANUARY – All the Sisters with Mr Prendergrast, Mr Kenworthy and myself went by the 9.20 ferry to Salonica, took a tram as near as we could to the Citadel, then walked over the hills to the back of the town onto the 3rd ridge near the foot of which was a (Turkish?) village. We had lunch on top of the 2nd. The air was delightful, the wind rather too strong at times. We found yellow, blue and white crocus. On our return we came down through the Arch in the wall to St Demetrius Church, 5th century (while that of St Georges was 3rd or early 4th). We took our lunch, so did not return till the 5 o/c ferry having had a very pleasant day.

5th JANUARY – A quiet day on board, a lovely sunny day.

6th JANUARY – Wet day, went on shore by the 1.20 ferry went to St George's and several other churches and mosques. Shops closed as it is the Greek Xmas. Heard the Kaiser was wounded.

7th JANUARY – Misty, but cleared later. We had a good service, well attended at 10.30.

8th JANUARY – Showery, so did not go ashore. Heard the Greeks had refused the Allied terms and that we had given 48 hours notice.

9th JANUARY – Miss Wilson princ. Matron came on board to lunch, afterwards made a tour of the wards, declared everything looked so clean and smart. At 1pm just as we were going into lunch an enemy aeroplane came over, our guns on shore and on sea fired but did not hit it, it was so high up, some went very close to it. It disappeared only to return later while we were at lunch, but only a few shots were fired when it disappeared. Went ashore with Miss Wilson in the launch, found out that Dr Morrish (Captn) of Streatham was stationed up country. He is attached to 17th Motor Amb. Convoy Lambeth. I spoke to him on the phone. He hoped to see me next time we are in. (Heard of the 'Cornwallis' sunk in the Mediterranean – 13 men missing).

10th JANUARY – A very wet day.

11th JANUARY – Went ashore at 9.00am with Lts Prince and Scott. Hunting for old black pottery and buying furs. The 'Ben-ma-Cree' sunk, 1 Off and 14 men wounded. Wing Commander Samson on board in the Med. The 'Cornwallis' was off Malta.

12th JANUARY – Very rough weather, cleared towards evening. In the evening the O/C Captn Barker, 4 Sisters and myself went to a dramatic entertainment on the 'Lord Nelson'. There were about 1,300 present. Lord and Lady Grenville, the new British representative of Venizuelos Govt were present, as was Admiral Thursby (Sir Cecil). The play was entitled 'The girl in the flat' – a musical comedy. It was an excellent entertainment. We were fetched by Mr J Ashford, who took us in No 1 pinnace, used by Lord Kitchener on his visit to the Peninsula, it still had the dainty little curtains which the bo'sain had put up for him. We retd at 10.15pm having had a most enjoyable evening.

13th JANUARY – Invitation from the 'Herefordshire' to a concert this evening. Our boys & theirs are having the 1st heat, boat race at 3pm. Our boys won the boat race today by 30 seconds. We were all ready for the concert, when the Captn said that the boats could not be lowered owing to a strong breeze which had sprung up, so we did not go. 'Letitia' filling & 'La France'.

14th JANUARY – Orthodox Greek's New Year's Day so a salute of 21 guns were fired at sunrise. The 'Minnetonka' came in filled with British troops about 9.00am. At 12.00 –12.50pm 7 aeroplanes were seen over the harbour, 6 of them very high up, we could not distinguish to what nation they belonged. Miss Clarke & Sis Jardin from the 'Herefordshire' came to tea and had a look over the 'Dover Castle'. A French troop ship came in, crowded. The 'H.S. Wandilla' came in.

Italian band played on shore, also the Greek band in honour of New Year's day. The 'Lord Nelson' went out. The 'Triad' staff and crew of which Mr Ashford belonged, left the 'Lord Nelson' yesterday for their own boat which had finished repairs. The weather colder, but bright. The snow, lower down on the hills, but not thick.

15th JANUARY – The 2nd part of the boat race between our orderlies and those of the 'Herefordshire' our boys won by 53 seconds. We are all invited to the concert on the 'Herefordshire' as it was put off the other night owing to our none appearance. We went to the 'Herefordshire' and thoroughly enjoyed ourselves. The concert was exceedingly good. After it we had refreshment and retd to the 'Dover' at about 12.00 midnight. The boys rowed us there and back.

17th JANUARY – The 'Panama' people joined us in a walking paper chase over the hills, the hares (4) had 20 minutes to get away, the hounds then followed about (20 in number) the hares were caught about 12.30. We had a very enjoyable time. The 'Herefordshire' were to join, but they left on the 16th for Stavros. Col. Emmerson sang well and he and Miss Clarke were excellent as host and hostess. Major Martin from the 'Panama' and Mr Drake joined us as hounds. A hostile air ship came over, but after a few shells left.

18th JANUARY – Heard that Captn Freestone (Chaplain of the 38th Gen) had been sent to the front and was killed by a bomb or shell from hostile aeroplane. The 'Herefordshire' returned from Stavros.

19th JANUARY – Left by the 9.00am ferry to see the Epiphany of the Cross. There was a high Festival in St Demetrius and in St Sophia to commemorate the baptism of our Lord. A Font is placed in the centre isle and decorated with ever greens, oranges and golden doves. A silver cross is blessed with water, then the congregations are sprinkled. When this part of the ceremony is over the people struggle to get near the water, almost fighting to get at it. The priests then start off to the white tower with the cross, about 8 priests in the procession in the gold and white. Great crowds witness the ceremony at the water's edge. At the pier, the priests and few others proceed to the end and after some little ceremony the cross is thrown into the water (3 doves loosed first, which fly away) and 19 men dive for it. The successful man was allowed to carry it round the town and collect money which he kept, so there was much struggling in the water and many lost their lives over it. In consequence of this, the priests threw the cross in and drew it out with a ribbon which was attached to it so no diving was allowed. After this ceremony the waters in the Gulf are deemed safe for a year. Last year a cross was lost at (…?…) and the city was lost on that account it is said, so if lost it means disaster. We went on the hills near the quarry to have lunch, then proceeded to the mosque near St Demetrius to see the Dervish dance. Mr & Mrs Michckophilaus accompanied us, the former is the Greek protestant minister here and his wife was a Scotch Missionary. The dance was not worth going to see, they have a circle of white goat skins a man sits, stands or kneels on one of these, then for about an hr they chant monotonously. Then the head one takes a kind of tom-tom, one starts singing, they all start swaying backwards, forwards and sideways and bobbing up and down, one stands in the middle and they all imitate him. They were mostly old men with quavering shrill voices, but got very hot in their exertions, poor things. We went to tea at the Michckophilaus' & were entertained well (15 of us).

20th JANUARY – Wet morning. Went to call on Mrs Jackson. She and her husband are the agents for this and all the principal lines, which usually means if anyone is left behind they are supposed to look after them till they have been sent on. This they had done for Sisters Mullen and Collyer, two of my Sisters who on the 16th went for a long walk with Padre Howard and missed the ferry. Their punishment (this was the 3rd time they were late) being that they were not allowed on shore for a day unless with a party of us. Mr & Mrs Jackson seemed very charming people. They have a son at the front acting as interpreter. Had a pleasant afternoon with them. Theirs is the only real English family in Salonica and it was truly good to be in an English home.

21st JANUARY – Mr Ashford (Asst pay master) came to take us to tea on 'H. S Triad'. He took us there in the pinnace and had asked several of his friends aboard to meet us. They had a very pretty and dainty table and we all had a very jolly time after tea sitting round a coal fire chatting.

22nd JANUARY – Snow on the lower hills today. It is very cold. I did not go to the 'Panama' paper chase as it was so cold, I thought I ought not to risk making my cold worse. We recd yesterday an invitation from Lt Dickinson to visit the 'E 14' tomorrow. On the 19th we heard that the captured German aeroplane which had been brought down intact was to be escorted down to the Mikra Bay aerodrome, by 2 English planes.

23rd JANUARY – The Sisters went on board the '*E 14*' in the afternoon. There were 8 Sisters and myself. Lt Dickinson fetched us in a pinnace and brought us back. It was very interesting, the propellers of a torpedo swung ready for the tube, were set in motion for us to see the double propellers at work, one going one way and the other the opposite. Everything was so spotlessly clean and so bright and every inch of room used. It looked very complicated and confusing to us, but everything necessarily in such order. The cooking was done for everyone in a stove about the size of an ordinary gas stove, but was heated by electricity, as was the boiler. The beds were like a chest of drawers drawing out and the tables also were ledges drawn out. There were tubes at either ends and in the middle they opened by the top half and the tube was lowered in and forced out by compression. There were 2 periscopes through which we could see our boat and recognise the others quite plainly. They were slightly diminished in size. We all had tea on '*H. M. S. Adamant*' the parent ship, we were joined by Lt (…?…) and a friend of Sis Collyer's, Captn Wilson, who had followed her from our boat having to sail the next day (Staff and crew on the '*E 14*' were 30).

24th JANUARY – Our Orderlies played the sailors of the '*E 14*' – goals 0-0. The '*Landovery Castle*' came in with a number of Sisters who were put off later.

25th JANUARY – One of the S. Western Railway Channel Steamers came in having collided with another ship, the bows very badly smashed down to the waters edge, she appeared to be sinking fast, but they moored her to a torpedo boat and a tug towed her along side the '*St George*' where they took off her cargo. It is said that the Admiral's ship the '*H. S. Triad*' was the one with whom she was in collision. The hole which was on the star board bow looks as though she herself was to blame. A large number of troop ships have come in since we have been here. A large ship full of Russians came in this morning. It is still very cold.

27th JANUARY – The '*Panama*' went out (not full) the '*Asturias*' went out full of French pts. The '*Minnetonka*' came in full of British troops.

29th JANUARY – Heard we were taking patients on next day. The '*H.S. Valdevia*' came in.

30th JANUARY – Took 155 pts on including 12 Off mostly medical. '*Herefordshire*' came in.

1st FEBRUARY – Took on 165 pts including 6 Officers.

2nd FEBRUARY – Wet cold day.

3rd FEBRUARY – Recd 142 pts including 8 Officers, 11 Sisters, 2 only of the latter are patients, the others on leave. Heard of Germany's proposal or rather statement, that she would sink all our ships at sight.

4th FEBRUARY – Heard America had broken off all negotiations with Germany, as she would not be dictated to re – her ships goings & comings.

5th FEBRUARY – Recd 132 pts including Officers 10, Sisters 5. Wireless Philadelphia America seized 2 aux cruisers & 4 merchant ships, the crews imprisoned in isolated barracks. 'E 14' went out 9pm. We left Salonica at 4pm beautiful sunny day & calm sea. We went nearer to the coast quite different to our usual course. About 11pm heard by wireless that an enemy submarine had been sighted on the route where we had been 5 hrs previously.

6th FEBRUARY – (Tuesday) Beautiful morning, sea very calm, till about 4 o/c, a strong wind came up suddenly & the sea was quite rough causing rolling & tossing at the same time, with the result – that nearly everyone was ill more or less. Even those who had never been ill before, partly through being still so long in Sala & partly through the suddenness of it.

7th FEBRUARY – Still rough, as it had been most of the night, but the wind whistled more softly. Squally at times, but many thankful that it was so, as we are less likely to encounter sub damages. Many of the patients are very ill, but seem to have improved a little since coming on board.

8th FEBRUARY – Warmer, patients improving each day.

9th FEBRUARY – Arrived off Malta very early, but did not get in to the harbour till after 12 o/c, disembarked 2.15 – 4.15. Lord Methuen & his son came on board, about 1pm.
    At 2 o/c the O/C – Maj Pemberthy & myself recd an invitation to dinner at 8.30pm that day. We had a pleasant evening with them at the old palace. The drawing room is especially handsome in its size & furniture. Walls are

Lord Methuen.

covered with red silk tapestry, the bulk of the furniture is upholstered in red silk. The ceiling is very handsomely painted & embossed. We were told of a French steamer in one of the harbours being on fire, they had to torpedo it & sink her, owing to her cargo of ammunition. Origin of fire not known (? treachery). On our journey from Sal they had recd news of 4 submarines. Recd letters & parcels.

10th FEBRUARY – Coaling. Went ashore in the morning. The fiesta of the anniversary of St Paul's shipwreck was being held. We went to St Paul's the Cathedral, which was decorated for the occasion. We also went to St John's. After lunch we went ashore again, did some shopping, had tea at the club. The B.R.C.S. commissioner M.Lefebre asked me to accept the use of his season ticket, for myself & friend, for the opera that evening to see 'Mde Sans Gene'. We, Sister Rothwell & I, enjoyed it immensely, Mde Bonaparte & (…?…) were excellent in their singing & acting, the former a little shrill in her high notes. Padre Prendergrast had succeeded in getting a ticket & so was with us.

11th FEBRUARY – Went ashore to return the ticket. We left Malta at 11am. Colder out of the harbour & a little rough. At night we recd wireless of a ship in distress off Marseilles, too far away for us to help.

12th FEBRUARY – Delightful weather, busy with my Red X stores. At 6pm recd wireless S.O.S. ship about an hr away to W. turned but just before arriving, recd another message "escaped, submarine shelled only", so we turned & went on our course. Lt Scott & I saw a sudden light about 3 miles off our starboard side which disappeared as suddenly but was not seen again.

13th FEBRUARY – Not so warm.

14th FEBRUARY – Arrived in Sala at noon. The 'Landovery', 'Gloucester Castle', 'Valdivia' & 'Herefordshire' in the 2nd filling. Cold.

15th FEBRUARY – Very cold morning. Sent letters home, went ashore in the afternoon.

16th FEBRUARY – Air raid about 4 o/c but shots no where near the planes, which soon got away.

17th FEBRUARY – Captn Flewitt came to lunch. Very pleasant bright day.

18th FEBRUARY – Miss Hall, Matron of the *'Valdivia'* came to lunch. *'H.M.S. Doris'* came in.

19th FEBRUARY – Went to see our men play football with the men from *'H.S. Endymion'* on the 43rd ground. The *'Endymion'* played a fine game, our men were kept hard at it, but could not get a goal till the last 3 minutes so it ended 9 – 1, Sellens scored.

20th FEBRUARY – To go to the *'Valdivia'* for a quoit tournament in the afternoon. Played quoit tournament & won every game with our quoits but lost all but one with theirs, which were rope & 55ft distance. We arrived back here about 6.20, dressed, had dinner, then went to a review on the *'Herefordshire'* given by their staff (a very good sketch). The *'H.S. Wandilla'* came in yesterday, bringing the only survivors of an Italian transport. 5 who were found on a raft. They say they had been on it 2½ days without food or water. They were escorted as far as the Adriatic Gulf & then left. Shortly after the escort left, she was torpedoed & sunk before any boats could be lowered. 1,100 troops were lost. We met Captn Staverly of the *'Endymion'* at the concert & several of the *'Doris'* Officers.

21st FEBRUARY – Cold wet day, went ashore to get a few things for our review. The *'H.M.S. Lord Nelson'* came in. Recd letter from home.

23rd FEBRUARY – The Princ. Matron & Miss Hall came to lunch. 2.30 our men had a boat race with the *'Valdivia'* & lost, 3 lengths. We gave our return tournament with Sisters & Officers of the *'Vala'* drew sets, 1 game to the good for us.

24th FEBRUARY – The *'Asturias'* came in, we with the Sisters & Officers from *'Herefordshire'* & *'Wandilla'* had a paper chase on the hills. We had a lovely day. On our return found Mr Wilcox (our C of E padre) had sailed for Marseilles. Went to the *'Endymion'* to a concert which was very good indeed. Lt Barnish & Mr Harris, paymaster, invited us. Lt Commander Staverly took me down to supper. *'Vala'* went to Stavros.

25th FEBRUARY – No service as we had not a padre. Enemy aeroplane over.

26th FEBRUARY – Wind very cold, sun warm. The *'Vala'* retd from Stavros about 5.30pm. Miss Sinclair Matron of the *'Neuralia'* came to arrange with me for our tennis tournament on Wednesday.

27th FEBRUARY – A lovely bright day. At 2.30 our R.A.M.C. men raced the *'Herefordshire'* & won, 50 sec. The stewards did the same with their stewards. At about 3.30pm I counted 11 enemy aeroplanes over, Captn Wilford counted 12 & it is said there were 15. They dropped bombs over the Monastir Rd of Salonica, we saw the smoke arise after the reports. One seemed to be hit, but righted itself & apparently all escaped.   (20 in all – 5 had been brought down above Salonica. (Air raid – 15) 170 killed & about 300 casualties).

28th FEBRUARY – Had our 1st boat out & enjoyed our rowing, called at the *'Neuralia'* & *'Herefordshire'* to arrange about the hockey match for tomorrow & Tuesday & the tennis for Monday. Have just heard that the casualties from air raid yesterday were 500 casualties & 170 killed (1 Sister hit badly in the jaw). The men were at manoeuvres in Summer Hill camp when the 15 planes came over, that is why so many were killed (1 aeroplane brought down).

1st MARCH – Very cold, snow on the hills.

2nd MARCH – Invitation to the *'Wandilla'* but the concert was put off till the 6th.

3rd MARCH – Still very cold out of the sun.

4th MARCH – Several aeroplanes came over in the night. At 8.15am 5 came over & dropped bombs on the 29th Gen Hos, the A.S.C. camp & the A.O.D. camp, none reached the munition dump near, which is the largest here. Two machines brought down before arriving at these camps (1 Sister killed ?) from 30 – 40 killed & many casualties. Father Prendergast & Kenworthy went to see the damage, brought a piece of shell for me & took some fine photos.

5th MARCH – Tennis (deck) with the *'Neuralia'* Sisters. Played & won 7 – 2. Major Sellar their O/C came over with padre & Captn Stephenson. The enemy came over (1 machine) at 2pm dropped a note over the 29th G.H. giving them 24 hrs to clear out. Went for a row.

6th MARCH – The 29th G.H. moved early, (the Sisters – patients). It was divided up between all the other hospitals. Our Sisters were to play the Seaforth Highlanders at hockey, but when we arrd at the ground, learnt that they had been sent hurriedly up country. Watched the S.W.H. & Navy play, & our men play football with the *'Neuralia'* 0-0. In the evening went to an entertainment on the *'H.S. Wandilla'*, all the Officers from the *'Lord Nelson'*, *'Doris'*, & *'St George'* the Italian flag ship & all the H. Ships were there. It was an excellent one. The *'Asturias'* went out early morning & the *'Landovery Castle'* came in. *'Herefordshire'* took on 200. Had the boat out but I steered & crewed.

7th MARCH – Very pleasant morning. The *'Herefordshire'* taking on again. She went out same day. Went to see the Sisters play hockey, but the Seaforth Highlanders had gone up country. Saw Miss Wilson as we were going near her hut, she asked me to see her on Friday afternoon.

8th MARCH – Cold, rough day, no ferry, S.Avery sprained ankle.

9th MARCH – Saw Miss Wilson, had tea, then hurried to catch our launch at the English Quay. Took on 304 patients in the morning.

10th MARCH – Sea too rough for the ferry, we took on 283 pts & 2 Sisters on leave. Too rough for nominal roll to be called for, did not get sailing orders as expected for that day.

11th MARCH – We left Sala about 10am. Sea in harbour rather rough, but outside it was calmer. Sun bright, wind colder. Passed 2 ships (escorted at 4.45pm).

12th MARCH – Beautifully sunny day, sea very blue, wind cold. Wireless announcing fall of Baghdad into our hands at 5.30am on the 11th.

13th MARCH – Sea rough, warmer, but wind cold. Stormy all night.

14th MARCH – Sea rough, showery at times, arrived at about 2pm. Disembarked patients, Sis Bilton & Tindall came (the former had a little pain).

15th MARCH – Saw Miss Beedsmore-Smith, went to the Red X (both). Did some shopping, after lunch went to the museum where I learnt more about the Island in its pre historic days or rather B.C. except for its stone & old earthenware & old jewellery, nothing much of interest. There were models of the old Temples. In the evening went to the opera which was very good as regards the music, the solos, duets & orchestra were really very, very good. The piece was 'i Zingari'. I heard 3 submarines had been caught off Malta 2 days ago. (see 28th March re 'Asturias')

16th MARCH – Left Malta at 10am, sea rather rough, wind cold, sun bright.

17th MARCH – Similar weather. St Pat's day.

18th MARCH – Wind strong & very cold as in the night. Another Sunday & no service for us.

19th MARCH – Wind still very cold. Transport 'Cashmine' at our stern all night with her escort (from Alex). She went ahead during the morning & kept there with the destroyer right into the harbour at Sala full of troops. Arrived Salonica.

20th MARCH – Our new C of E Padre-Davis came on board from 'Cashmine'. Mr Grant R.C.C. came on also (temp). A mail came on.

21st MARCH – Lt Hayne came on, he informs us that there was an air raid up country over the 36th & 37th G.H. (used for Serbs) & that 2 Sisters were killed. This occurred the day we left 11/3/17, there were 28 machines they were turned at Vertikof.

22nd MARCH – Went to the 29th where nearly all the tents had been removed to Mikre Bay, saw many of the holes made by the shells fired from enemy planes on the 27th. Sea choppy.

23rd MARCH – Went to see Miss Wilson pm who came back to lunch with me. Lovely day.

24th MARCH – 'Wandilla' arrived at 8am.

26th MARCH – 'Wandilla' went to Stavros.

27th MARCH – Took on 237 pts. including 2 Off.

28th MARCH – Wireless of the loss of the 'Asturias' (H.S.) torpedoed in the Channel on the 21/3/1917 with all lights fully on. 11 med. staff killed, 3 missing including 1 staff nurse, 17 injured, 20 crew killed, 9 missing including 1 stewardess, 22 injured. No patients on board at the time. Took on 164 pts.

29th MARCH – Took on 181 including 12 Officers & 1 Sister (traveller). Left Salonica at 3.40pm. Lovely day. Many wounded on board, also trench feet, med cases – Malaria & rheumatism chiefly.

30th MARCH – Lovely day, passed all the islands except Crete by 8pm.

31st MARCH – Lovely weather, sea calm, passed 'H.S. *Valdivia*' away on the horizon about 9.20am she was going East.

1st APRIL – Arrived in Marsa Sirocco about 11.45am left shortly after, did not anchor, arrived Malta about 2pm. Went on shore in the evening saw Miss Bilton who was in Sick Sisters Hosp. – severe cold & neuralgia.

2nd APRIL – Went to Head Qrts. & B.R.C.S. office, shopped, then went to San Antonio Palace to lunch with Lord & Lady Methuen & family, one o/c & R.C Chaplain Mr Rigby went, met several others there. Was told of Miss McCarthy's illness & that Miss Beedsmore-Smith was appointed Matron in Chief B.G.F, Miss Osbourne to be P. M. of Malta. Saw them both. Had we gone home we were to take Miss Beedsmore-Smith with us, but we recd orders to proceed to Salonica at 5pm. Left Malta 5pm 2 B.R.C.S ladies with us, Miss Molson and Miss Westland, who are to proceed for duty to Salonique. Miss Westland lived in Ceylon (Kandy) for many yrs, has a brother in Colombo living at Colpetty.

5th APRIL – Nothing exciting happened on the journey, had SOS signal, but 50 miles off & arrived at Salonica in the afternoon just 7 days from when we left. We passed the '*Wandilla*' a day after we left Malta.

6th APRIL – When to see Miss Wilson (P.M.) & to the 43rd where we had tea, called at Mrs Jackson's, saw Miss Wilson on our way back, took a sailing boat from the white tower as I was afraid we might miss the ferry.

7th APRIL – Went to the Red X stores in the morning.

8th APRIL – Easter day – had had a very bad night, in pain all night, went to early service & then straight to bed where I remained until the 18th when I was allowed up for 1 hr on the sofa. We heard the '*H.S. Gloucester Castle*' had been torpedoed in the channel. All were saved including the wounded. This was confirmed by Berlin official on 11/4/17 – tord by a U boat on the 30th-31st.

9th & 10th APRIL – Still in pain & very little sleep.

11th APRIL – '*H.S. Salta*' sunk in the channel said to be mined during bad weather. Missing are 5 Off, 9 Sisters & 38 others. I had some beautiful wild flowers brought from the hills & more from the fields. On the hills are anemone, all colours, primroses, cowslips. I had poppies, wild oats, marguerites, marsh mallow & a small yellow flower very like a jasmine. I also had some fine daffs, anemone from the garden (& stocks) (very cold).

19th APRIL – Took 302 pts on, all windows blackened to have 2 escorts full & 1 when empty. '*H.S. Glengorn Castle*' 2 days overdue from Malta.

20th APRIL – Sat up for an hour. Very cold. News of 31,000 prisoners taken in France in 8 days by us.

21st APRIL – Very cold morning, sat up 1½ hrs. We heard the '*Arcadian*' was sunk & other hospital ship losses. The latter announced in Parliament by Bonar Law.

22nd APRIL – Hear that 2 more, '*Cameronian*' & another, are sunk. Cannot get any news of ourselves. It is thought generally that we may have to go ashore & the boat lie in Micra Bay. I went on deck for a short time in the afternoon.

23rd APRIL – Beautiful day, went on deck from 2.30 – 5.15 except while having tea in my cabin. 3 transports arrived with troops escorted by 3 destroyers. (2 French and 1 Italian ships full of troops).

24th APRIL – The '*H.S. Lanfranc & Dongola*' sunk in the channel. I was on deck for 3 hrs.

25th APRIL – The '*Lanfranc*' was full of patients, many wounded Prussian guard on board as well as our own men. The prisoners behaved very badly over the boats. I was on deck for several hrs, feeling stronger & rather more comfortable. We saw 8 aeroplanes going over towards Doiran front about 3.15pm they had not retd at 6pm so expect they were on business bent. Two others remained scouting all round.

26th APRIL – We heard that an important point on the Doiran-Vardar front had been attacked & won by us. Very cold wet day.

27th APRIL – Cold & wet.

28th APRIL – Lovely bright day, wind cold. We heard that the enemy had regained the new point, where we had nearly broken through their line on the Dor-Var front with very heavy losses on our side.

29th APRIL – Bright day – wind cold.

5th MAY – Still in Sala. Went on the 'H.S Wandilla' to see Miss Wilson Prin Mat.

7th May – Boarded as not been advisable for me to stay out here. We had the R.A.M.C. review to which were invited the 'St George' Officers – the 'Triad' N.T. Officers from shore, Princ Staff Off & Prin Matron, also the Officers & Sisters from Naval 'H.S. St Margaret', 'H.S. Landovery', 'Valdivia', 'Neuralia'. The review was a great success.

8th MAY – Sent off 145 pts, admitted 164, total left on board 320 all for home.

9th MAY – (Recd approv) re-the board on me, but feel very much better. We recd letters from home.

11th MAY – Recd (…?…) patients all for home. I went by launch to Brit: Hosp: Pier & from there to Miss Wilson to wish her goodbye. The flowers on the way were very pretty – poppies, daisies, veitch, convulvuli, marsh mallow & Sister Riley & I had tea at 11 o/c at the 5th Can. Hos. with Sis Dowding.

12th MAY – The Sisters all left at 10am & we sailed just after 2 o/c the 'T.B.D Foxhound' & 'Comet' accompanying us as our escorts on either side. Fire drill at 4.30pm. We had 5 stewardesses on – 1 from 'Valdivia', 1 from 'Landovery Castle' & 2 from 'Neuralia' besides our own.

13th MAY – Dull day, cold & wet at intervals. The '*T.B.D. Foxhound*' & '*Comet*' are certainly doing their duty splendidly, covering every bit of the road, one on either side a little in advance crossing our bows each time, their zigzag turning is towards us. Expecting to arrive at Soudhas Bay at midnight, when our splendid escort will get a little much needed rest. Discovered one of the 2 '*Neuralia*' stewardesses is Miss Green from the old transport & '*Avoca*' (B.India).

14th MAY – We arrived in Soudhas Bay, Crete about 11.45pm, very dark & stormy. Woke up this morning to see a beautiful blue harbour surrounded by high green hills, the nearest over 2,000 ft high. The island is 148 miles long & (...?...) wide, 320,000 inhabitants, Candia is the capital. There is a town near 4 miles Khania. Cold showery day.

15th MAY – Much brighter day, but wind cold. Some of the Officers went ashore & brought some lovely roses, honeysuckle & a large red lily back looking quite as if from home. We took 3 patients on – one a skipper who had been left in hospital with dysentery, the transport having to go, (he had been torpedoed 12 months ago off Marseilles). One was atropine & the other wounded, both from the '*Arcadia*' which was torpedoed going from Sala to Alex. There are others in hosp having lost their limbs. The '*Huntsend*' is beached here but they have repaired her sufficiently to go to Malta. She was a German boat now taken over by the Union Castle Lines. Since she was torpedoed they have used her as a sort of hotel for crews of other torpedoed ships.

16th MAY – Showery. Our escorts the sloops '*Marguerite*' & the '*Beri-Beri*' came in in the morning. We left at 6.30pm I had an invitation from Sis Goldstraw of the '*Thelirius*' to go to see her. She is the flagship & repair ship for Crete for all the allies. Also an invitation from Lt Commander Turner to tea & see over his boat the '*Marguerite*', but postponed it to Malta. He sent me a large bunch of flowers by Major (...?...) & Mr Harris. We passed by the wreck of the '*Minnewoska*' as she lay on her side on the rocks, after she was beached. It was a sad sight to see such a fine ship in such a condition. It was just outside the boom.

17th MAY – A lovely fresh day & the sea blue & calm.

18th MAY – A lovely fresh day, arrived in Malta at about 2pm. The embarkation officer Major Hamilton did not know we were coming till we were in, I was disembarked at 3pm for Sister's Hosp. as patient. Just as I was disembarking 2 wires were brought to me I stopped, opened one telling me of father's death on the 3rd May, the 2nd which should have been 1st telling me of the stroke. My last letter told of how busy he was in his garden, it was of course a great shock to me. I went to bed as soon as I could, everyone was most kind here altho strangers.

19th MAY – Miss May Thorne examined me, as she is the M.O. here, pronounced my heart sound, liver beautiful, lungs good except crepitus at apex of left lung (back) where I had pleurisy 17 yrs ago, my spleen normal, said evidently inflammation had subsided very much, but advised an operation in London if not subsided still more on my arrival. I went out in the afternoon saw Mr Doherty & Scott & other ship's Officers. Scott wished me to call to see his wife if possible when in London (to go to Wimbledon). I returned about 5pm (after 2 hrs) feeling very tired & glad to go to bed. Miss Osbourne was in to see me in the morning, they will do their best to get me away on Tuesday the 22nd.

20th MAY – Miss Hall came to see me & I went to tea in the afternoon feeling not quite so well. Sr Bilton came for a $\frac{1}{4}$ of an hr.

21st MAY – Walter Tallis came to see me. His 'T.B.D. Redpole' in harbour he has 4 days leave & so he is spending it at the Melita Hotel, San Antonio. He arranged for Sr Bilton & I to have tea there with him then we went in the fine old gardens. I went to Head Qrtrs & learn that there was not any vacancy so I cannot get home before the end of the month anyhow.

22nd MAY – I went by train to St. Antonio, Walter met me at the station. We went into the gardens & had tea at the hotel.

23rd MAY – Just as I was booking for Attars I saw two patients from our last trip, Major (…?…) & Captn Hunter going to Citta Vecchia when we got into the train there were Lt Scott & Padre Davis. Walter met me at the stn then we went to Mosta to see the 3rd largest dome in the world. The church was built about 50 yrs ago is octagonal, the dome extending all over the church.

There are a few old pictures from the former church which stood for 3 centuries. We returned to the hotel for tea. On our way out we went into an old mill & saw them grinding corn & separating the flour.

Mosta Church
– circa 2002.

It, after grinding, was put into a long cylindrical tube made of fine gauze, which caused the finest flour to fall when turned. What was left was then put into another causer, when what appeared to be chaff was left. After tea we went into the gardens, when hearing myself called from behind I turned to see our 2nd Off. & the Purser from the 'Dover Castle' they told me that they are embarking patients on the D.C. tomorrow & 11 o/c so I must ask if there is a chance for me to go. We all stayed together till time to go back in the train.

24th MAY – Went to see Miss Hall in the afternoon, it was Empire day, the scouts all met at Floriana Square & marched to the Palace Square for inspection. There were several hundreds all looking very smart.

25th MAY – Went for a motor drive round the coast, passing nearly all the hospitals & convalescent camp. We went throu Antifia (a very pretty fertile valley) & round by St Pauls Bay, Mitarpa, Mosta, St. Antonio, Birchicana & Sliemma. Here & there the rocks were very barren, but one realises the extent of the island & its cultivation on such a drive. The coast was fine also. The 'Dover Castle' & 'Karapara' went out (2 T.B.D. for escorts) at 11.30am.

26th MAY – Not quite so well, had a day in bed. 'Dover Castle' torpedoed, hear she is beached off Algiers, some reports say 60 missing, others that all are saved. I hope the latter is true. All safe.

27th MAY – Went out with Walter Tallis for a short time in the evening into the gardens at Floriana (Sunday). 'H.S. Goorkha' is in harbour.

28th MAY – Recd answer to my application to be sent home as soon as possible. Earliest date 10th – 17th June. Met Matron Hall in the evening.

29th MAY – Went for a shampoo in the morning, rested in the afternoon. Some 6 Sisters sick from the 'H.S. Wandilla' came in the afternoon. She had come from Sala, her staff of Matron and Sisters were put off day of leaving Sala they got the news of the 'Dover Castle' while at Crete & I hear are to take the survivors onto England. General Yarr came & confirmed the news about home.

30th MAY – Miss Hall came to see me. I went to examine the 'Dover Castle' mail bags, 12 by permission of authorities under the eye of the O/C only found 2, the others having gone to Sala so had not had any news. The 'H.S. Wandilla' went out just as I was returning to the shore, to pick up the survivors of the *'Dover Castle'*. I went for a short walk with Walter.

2nd JUNE – Walter Tallis & I went to Marsa Scala by ferry, Karrozzin to the beach, then walked round the point. We came upon salt basins cut out of the rocks, they had been gathering the salt by sweeping with small besoms (about 6 in long) & by scraping with wooden butter pats then they filled them with water again (the tide did not come so far in) so the water apparently drained away or evaporated gradually, leaving the salt. The people engaged, built hovels of stone from the shore, had a little fire stove of stone & a few cooking utensils, that was all we could see. We moved on a little more & sat down to our tea, which we had taken with us, enjoying it, after which we returned the same way having spent a very pleasant afternoon.

4th JUNE – Went for a drive in the B.R.C.S. car.

5th JUNE – Went to tea with Miss Hall at Floriana.

6th JUNE – Went out a little in the evening with Walter Tallis.

7th JUNE – Sr Bilton came.

9th JUNE – Walter & I went to Bersi-Bugge for tea. We drove out to the rocks then went for a short walk & rested on the rocks enjoying a fresh breeze.

Birzebbuga (Bersi –Bugge) – circa 2002.

We had tea at the hotel on the balcony over the sea, drove back 5.45 having had a very pleasant afternoon. John's birthday. Order came for big baggage.

10th JUNE – Bad attack of colic so was kept in bed till Monday aft. Had not felt so well for several days.

11th JUNE – Rather better, but Dr would not consent that I should have charge of the party.

12th JUNE – Orders for embarking at 6.30am on the 13th (on the 'Isonzo') W.T. came & we had a walk.

13th JUNE – Transport late did not go till 7 o/c. The 'Isonzo' cut along at 24 knots hr. We left at 9.45am we had plenty of movement as she rides the waves instead of cutting through. We arrived at Syracuse about 3.15am. There was an oil steamer called 'The Mitra' which had been torpedoed (next to us) & hear her bows had nearly sunk to the waters edge, they were pumping away, 2 boats besides themselves. We stayed the night at the Hotel L'Estrange, arising at day break. We drove round the town & to the Capuoccini gardens & the old Greek caves or tombs & prisons. We were very tired.

14th JUNE – Called at 4.30am bkft at 5.30, left at 5.45 for the station. We had a 6 hr run then embarked on the ferry at Messina. The ferry had 4 guns and 8 gunners on. We crossed the gulf to Si Giovanni then entrained for Rome.

15th JUNE – At Rome here we stayed for 12 hrs & I took some of the Sisters to St Peters, Vatican, Sistine Chapel, Coliseum, Forum Rom & the Pincis. We drove early. We had tea at Miss Rabingtons, she came in as did Misses Snell & Watney & so we all had a chat. We put up at the Grand Hotel Continental. We left at 11.15 having the whole carriage, with the exception of one compartment given to the naval officers, who were on the 'Isonzo' with us, some shipwrecked & others on leave. The Matron, Sisters & VAD's of our party were 25. We heard that one of the bridges we had crossed the evening before was torpedoed.

16th JUNE – Very hot all day. The country everywhere is lovely, there is much movement among the soldiers everywhere. I saw an airship in the afternoon scouting east, the early morning some heliographing. Arrived Genoa about noon, bought lunch & took with us. We all had to change at Modane, but managed to keep our compartment the whole way, Sister C. Maskell, Staff N's Woodford &Tompkins, with myself. The train rocked very bad.

17th JUNE – Very hot day – arrived Paris about 10.30am put up at the Grand Hotel du Lourve. Everyone felt at the end of their tether so had breakfast & went to bed, till tea was brought at 4 o/c. We bathed, dressed & went for a drive to get some air without adding to our fatigue along the Bois du Boulogne. It all looked so fresh & bright, but very different to the ord. Sunday in Paris.

18th JUNE – Slept splendidly till about 6 o/c then dosed on & off till 8.45am ordered bkft then bathed dressed & went to the Consuls, after to the provost Marshal, who arranged for our journey for the rest of the way. Cptn Stockwell was exceedingly kind came to the Stn Gard du Nord to see us comfortably settled & keep everyone else away. In the evening after tea (we had rested in the afternoon) went to the Notre Dame. We left the hotel at 10 o/c at night. Arrived Boulogne about 9.30am.

19th JUNE – Had bkft at Hotel Du Louvre Boulogne, went a run in the tram Wim Veuse, made enquiries at 13th G.H. for the Parkes, saw Miss Stuart, a regular Sister, who had been with them at 14th Gen. I heard Mrs P. had gone to 14th Sta a little further up & Joyce had gone home. We left Boulogne by the 'S.S. *Victoria*' at 2pm arrived a Folkestone at 3.50 & at Victoria Stn about 6.45pm. We then came to Sister's Hospital, Vincent Square, SWW1.

20th JUNE – I saw Major Charles Worth who is boarding me for leave on urgent ptc business affairs after which I am to return & go to Millbank hosp. arranging with them when I can come back. I saw Mr Dick of the R.N.P.F. for nurses & paid up till March 1st 1918. Wire to sis.

21st JUNE – Rested in the morning writing letters, in the afternoon went to the Comd Paymaster, returning shortly after 3 to find Mr Warner waiting for me. It was very pleasant to see & chat with him once more. He stayed to tea. I thought he was looking much thinner. In the evening D. Salt came. I sent off my pay book and travel claims.

22nd JUNE – Leave for 3 weeks given, went to Shirley. Howard & Nelly met me at B'ham & drove me home. Very tired, but pleased to get safely in.

23rd JUNE – Clive came, having passed his exam, to wait till he was gazetted.

25th JUNE – Joe & Kath went home with me to Sutton to pack up and go through papers, letters etc & Mr Rudd came in the afternoon & stayed to tea. It did not seem like home without father.

26th JUNE – Joe left us after dinner. Kath & I found I could not finish that day, Mrs Showells helped us, Mr Rudd came to tea. Howard & Nelly came later & took things back with them.

27th JUNE – Kath & I left about 6pm for Shirley feeling absolutely done. I rested till 3rd July.

2nd JULY – Eric came home, he came up to The Grange to tea. Lizzie S also came & Sam in the evening.

The Grange, Shirley, Warwickshire.

3rd JULY – I went home as the lorry was going to Sutton for the things we wished to keep. After they had gone I finished father's papers etc & I called Dr Evans, had tea & a chat with him & then left for Shirley very very tired (I called in the cemetery, the inscription not done).

6th JULY – Went home to see the old home dismantled, took a walk round the garden for the last time & came away feeling very broken, hoping I should not meet anyone. I recd a letter saying they had vacant bed for me, would I come to Millbank for the opera.

7th JULY – Feeling quite done, but eventually packed & went arriving about 9pm for I could not get a cab at Paddington for nearly an hour. I had a dull little room to myself, but felt rather glad to be alone. There had been one of the largest & worst air raids in the morning in London.

11th JULY – Had my operation for haemorrhoids, never knew anything till I came round in the room & saw my locker. In the afternoon I was moved into a bright airy ward for 2, the Sisters sharing it being one of the former Panama Sisters, Mrs Puller from S.A. Very sick all night, but fairly easy, but scarcely slept at all. Miss Bond came to see me.

12th JULY – Sickness continued all day and night.

13th JULY – Sickness till afternoon when I had a little bread & butter, not sick after. Miss Bond came to see me.

14th JULY – B.O. (Bowels opened) first time, after enema & oil, pain, but not so bad as in April, but very sore.

17th JULY – Mrs Hynes came to see me.

18th JULY – No word of my baggage, afraid it has gone down, as we hear it left Malta on 26th June. Mr Hemsley, Purser of the D.C. came to see me & tell me about the sinking of the D.C. They were struck on the 26th May just under the dining Saloon at 3 mins past 7pm. The patients & R.A.M.C. behaved splendidly & all were got safely in the boats except 6 firemen who were killed. One fireman caught up another who was badly injured & carried him into safety eventually, though both were floating about in dirty water & came up with it dripping off them. The 'Camelion' (escort) came up & the patients & everyone were quickly transferred to her. After our Comdr & the Comdr of escort consulted & they agreed to ask for a few volunteers & Captn & Officers with these got back onto the D.C. as she was still floating, then the escort proceeded to Bona where she landed the rescued. Shortly after 8pm those on the D.C. felt another bang. They all managed to get into the only remaining boat & push off. The last torpedo shook her from bow to stern shaking Mr Hemsley off the lower part of rope into the boat & she went down in 4 minutes. 6 hrs later they were picked up by the 'Camelion' who had come back for them. 'Marcain Kenworthy' signalled to her when they saw her lights about 2.30am & very dark. I heard Mr Harris arrd in

England late in June & is to be Chief on a trooper. Williams, the 3rd, is on '*H. S. Gloucester Castle*' as 2nd, Linklater the chief, not apptd yet but taking a course of gunnery with Mr Chandler who is home. They are going up for a gunnery exam next week, then Mr Chandler to go as 2nd on a trooper.

19th JULY – Mr & Mrs Chandler came to see me, I felt brighter for seeing these old Doverites & chatting of old friends & acquaintances, both looked well.

20th JULY – Mr Fuller went to Vincent Square & another Sister C.A.M.C. (Mrs Mercer) came in perineal abscess.

21st JULY – Mrs M had operation. Sister Tompkin came to see me.

22nd JULY – Sunday – about 8.30am while waiting for bkft, but loud bang came & telephone warning, 'get all pts to basement' as there is an air raid. No mistaking it either, one seemed to have dropped almost on us, but I think did not do much damage. We were back in our wards about 9.20 for bkft, then later came another message 'prepare they are coming again'. However, our people drove them back. Mrs Mercer sent to Royal Free Hosp. so am alone once more.

23rd JULY – Mrs Dixon, Miss Levd & Nellie Hayne came to see me. I got up & sat in the chair after tea.

24th JULY – Dressed except dress & sat up from 4.15 – 7.30pm.

25th JULY – Dressed at 2pm.

26th JULY – Dolly Sale came to see me & I went out for 10 minutes.

27th JULY – Drove over to Oxford Street.

28th JULY – Went out for a walk, very tired.

29th JULY – Went to Vincent Square.

30th JULY – Mr & Mrs Chandler came, took me out to tea & to King & Co to see about my luggage. Very wet.

31st JULY – Very wet day. Had Med. Board, given 3 weeks leave.

1st AUGUST – Left Paddington at 11am for Dartmouth arriving about 5.30pm. Mrs Adams & Beatrice met me at Kingswear.

3rd AUGUST – Went to Paignton & Torquay.

6th AUGUST – Went for a picnic up the river.

7th AUGUST – Went onto their house boat 'The Frog'.

11th AUGUST – Went to Paignton to the Hut for tea.

13th AUGUST – Edie Adams & I went to Torquay.

14th AUGUST – Went to Mrs Hopkins, Kingswear to tea (very wet day).

15th AUGUST – Retd to London (39 Bedford Street, to Queen Mary's Hosp).

16th AUGUST – Went to War Office, did not see Miss Rickads saw Miss Hordley. Arranged Med. Board for next day at Vincent Square.

17th AUGUST – Med. Board.

18th AUGUST – Went to Kings to get things from my baggage at King & Co. Arrived at Shirley about 6pm.

19th AUGUST – Drove over to Joe's to fetch them to The Grange.

20th AUGUST – Went up town. Had dinner with John & Ada at The Beeches.

22nd AUGUST – Heard from the War Officer that my sick leave was extended to 6th September. Louie came & Ada.

25th AUGUST – Howard drove Nellie, Kath, Alice, Joan & I over to Droitwich to Lizzie's, Emily and Nora there. Had a pleasant ride.

29th AUGUST – Ada hired a motor & we drove over to Kenilworth.

9th SEPTEMBER – Went to a very interesting séance with Howard, Sis, Dr & Mrs Kath Kneale, Dr & Mrs Pollard & Dolly, Mrs Johnson.

(Here the diary ends)

Excerpt from Sue Wood: If we still had the rest of the diary, it would probably have contained the following entry on the next page:

'13th December – had Med Board. Passed fit for general service'. Service and duty seem to have been central to every decision Katy Beaufoy took. Her diary records her exhaustion prior to the haemorrhoids operation and that she was forced to rest at the end of June for nearly a week. Physically in pain, she was also depressed by the emptying of the house in Sutton Coldfield and her last visit there. Uncharacteristically, she records her feelings about the event. Nevertheless, during this bleak period she finds time to write to the Matron in Chief to inform her of her change of address, her father's death, her operation and most importantly she notes:

Paragraph 3 states that I should report to the War Office 10 days before expiration of leave. Is that necessary in my case? Major Charlesworth advised me to write to Milbank as soon as I had finished and was ready, and ask when there would be a vacancy.

I have the honour to be Madam

Your obedient Servant

K. Beaufoy.

How typical of her that she should be enquiring about a vacancy in spite of everything.

6. THE FINAL CHAPTER

After settling her father's affairs Katy was posted to Royal Victoria Hospital, Netley on 27th October 1917 but she was not happy and so she asked for another posting. On the 1st November 1917 she was appointed Matron of the British Hospital ship *'Glenart Castle'*.

'Glenart Castle' (from an original painting by Jeff Hollins – 2001).

The ship sailed on 25th February 1918 from Newport, South Wales, outward bound for Brest, France, without passengers. Katy now found herself a target; her own particular slavering 'dog of war' had detached itself from the pack. With endless patience Katy and *'Glenart Castle'* were hunted down, across oceans, until the ever-watchful creature was ready to pounce. On the 26th February, 1918 the ship was proceeding down the Bristol Channel when, at 4am, off Lundy Island (despite her being painted white with large green stripes and three Red Crosses on each side fully illuminated) she was torpedoed by the German submarine UC56. The hunter struck once in the lonely and hostile environment of a winter sea; it was enough – Katy was gone. The ship sank in 4 to 7 minutes with only 32 survivors out of a complement of 182. Captain Burt, all the Nursing Sisters, a female stewardess – Elizabeth Elbra and the two Chaplains were amongst those who lost their lives with Katy. As we have no diary pages after September 1917 we can only assume that the remaining part of the journal was lost with Katy in the Bristol Channel.

Under international law the submarine commander had the right to stop and search the ship to obtain proof of her status as a hospital ship. This he chose not to do, as was the case with most of the hospital ships sunk by submarines. The commander in question, one Wilhelm Kiesewetter, later took his boat into the Spanish port of Santander where he and his crew were interned. After the War he found passage in a Dutch ship bound for Germany. His transport had to make a scheduled call at Falmouth, where Kiesewetter promptly found himself under arrest for the sinking of 'Glenart Castle'. For reasons that we will never know, Kiesewetter had been issued with a safe conduct by a foreign diplomatic service. After two weeks of deliberation the British Government came to the conclusion that conduct must be honoured. Apart from official word that the ex submarine skipper had arrived in Germany that was the last ever heard of the man.

In July 2000 two members of Ilfracombe Sub Aqua Club, Keith Denby and Jack Stocks, took Gill Morgan and Joyce & Michael Harrison out to the lonely wreck site where Gill was able to drop a memorial plaque over the ship. At a dinner in Ilfracombe later that evening the conversation turned to thoughts of a permanent memorial to 'Glenart Castle' as there is no mention of her in the Devon shipwreck museums. After a lot of hard work, by Keith Denby in particular, a piece of land was donated; a stone was acquired and engraved. The memorial was erected at Hartland Point on February 26th 2002, the eighty-third anniversary of the sinking. The dedication was led by The Rev. Brian Bolt* and was attended by members of Katy's family; friends of Gill; members of Ilfracombe Sub Aqua Club, including Keith and Jack; Mrs Diana Price who gave the land; Hartland British Legion; Hartland school children and many local people.

Visitors who make the journey to Hartland Point will be rewarded with scenes of massive cliffs which soar to 350ft. People have been trekking to the point for thousands of years; the Romans were often here – they referred to the Point as "the Promontory of Hercules". To see the site of the sinking the visitor should stand directly facing the memorial. On a clear day visibility is about 21.3 miles and the ship lies 20 miles from the memorial.

* Deceased 2004.

'Iron Ghost' – The sinking of the Glenart Castle, and raising of the memorial

Hospital Ship 'Glenart Castle', torpedoed and sunk 26th February 1918.

For the sick and wounded of a war far from home, a hospital ship is a respite from pain and danger and the prospect of a return to family and loved ones. For those who serve on hospital ships, there is no respite, the work is immense and the danger is constant.

Hospital ships are unarmed, traditionally painted white with highly visible red crosses. At night they carry full navigation lights, with a green band all round the ship and with the red crosses illuminated – even in the darkest military blackout. In February 1918, the crew and medical staff of 'H.S. Glenart Castle' knew that the danger had increased as they left Cardiff on the afternoon of the 25th, bound for Brest to take on patients. Hospital ships were now a deliberate target of the desperate U-boats, thwarted and destroyed by the convoy system of the Allied navies. In January the 'H.S. Rewa' was torpedoed off the North Cornish coast whilst carrying wounded but fortunately almost everyone was rescued. The Matron of the 'Glenart Castle', Katy Beaufoy had served in the Boer War and for the whole of the Great War to date. She had cared for thousands of sick and wounded and had seen her share of dangers – she wrote in her diary in May 1917 "'Dover Castle' torpedoed, hear she is beached off Algiers. Some reports say 60 missing, others that all are saved. I hope that the latter is true". Katy Beaufoy was Matron of the 'Dover Castle' but was unwell at the time she sailed and did not go.

Evidence given at the Admiralty Court of Inquiry held on the 27th February 1918 is shown in appendices.

7. RAISING OF THE MEMORIAL

A storm of fearsome strength and laced with horizontal rain was tearing at the village when we arrived on Monday February 25th 2002. We had arrived a day early to avoid travel delays and most importantly to meet people who had given unstintingly of their time, as they became caught up in the project and the need to see it to fruition.

At the Somme Battlefield Gill Morgan had remarked that her great Aunt Katy had lost her life in a hospital ship that had been torpedoed off the coast of Ireland. Following up the lead soon revealed that the ship in question had been attacked off 'Lundy Island' and was known as *'Glenart Castle'*; a name we shall never forget. It soon became apparent that we needed expert local knowledge and a chance e-mail to Ilfracombe Sub Aqua Club put us in touch with Keith Denby and his friend Jack who were interested in the ship. Six months later in early July 2001 Gill, my wife Joyce and myself left Knowle early to rendezvous with Keith and Jack who were to take us out to the wreck site in their club boat, Neptune. Expressing our excitement is not easy; our eyes were glued to the sonar and global position system (GPS). We had none of us ever witnessed the like of what we saw that day, exactly as the GPS predicted the sonar image of the ship appeared; an iron ghost with a story to tell us. She reached out and touched us all 'tell people of me and those that I carried', an incredible moment which left a deep and lasting impression. Midway across the site Gill dropped a brass plate detailing the events of February 26th 1918. The attached sinker stones had been taken from the garden of what is now a housing estate in Shirley, Solihull where Katy lived with her sister following the death of her parents.

The evening of the 25th saw us once more braving the gale to meet the others of our party at the Anchor Inn. The hospitality and good food revived our spirits and we left the inn in good cheer to find the Royal British Legion and in particular President Peter Skinner, the long suffering recipient of our sometimes frantic telephone calls from Knowle. Peter moved mountains for complete strangers and like all others that we met, asked nothing in return.

Only nature herself could stop us, and this she seemed determined on. Most of our party were awoken by a howling wind in the very early hours of Tuesday. It was as though a fiend walked the streets of Hartland, banging on doors and windows for admittance. Long dark hours were spent on contingency plans for an alternative site for the following morning's ceremony. How could we take school children and people in their mid seventies up to Hartland Point where the roaring gale could easily blow mere humans away as it they were but straws in the wind? As has happened all through this project obstacles melted away, in this case the angry wind died, the sun began to shine and spirits soared.

We estimated that 60-70 people turned out for the Dedication including children from Hartland School. The chosen hymn was Eternal Father Strong to Save. The last two lines of each verse proved too much for me, I could feel liquid welling up behind my eyelids. A Royal Marine bugler, the Legion Standard Bearers and the Royal navy added colour and dignity to our service. As the two minutes silence was observed I noticed a gull wheeling just out to sea, it flew off when the bugler sounded reveille. Then it was all over. To us it seems incredible that it happened at all, one hears of similar projects taking several years to complete.

After lunch at Hartland Legion, short speeches and thanks, were given by members of Katy Beaufoy's family. Eighty-four years to the day they now have closure, the brave girl can rest in peace. Vicky Hollins, Knowle Legion Chairperson, donated a painting of the ship executed by her husband, Jeff. None of this would have come to pass had it not been for the kindness and generosity of the people of North Devon. You proved beyond doubt that the ugly creed of selfishness does not hold sway everywhere in these islands. Thank you and bless you.

And what of 'our' great ship, *'Glenart Castle'*? She sleeps the long silent slumber of lost ships everywhere.

We would like to thank the following; if I have omitted any names then you have my unreserved apologies.

Rev. Brian Bolt

Keith and Jack – Ilfracombe Sub Aqua Club

Peter Skinner – Hartland, Royal British Legion

The Legion Standard Bearer and his Lady counterpart who both gave up paid employment to be with us

The Royal Navy

Trinity House

The Royal Marines

Ilfracombe Harbour Master

Mr and Mrs Price who donated the site for the memorial

Hartland School

The Legion Club Steward who worked on his day off

Hilary Kirby for her excellent B&B

Nigel Stevens, who produced photographic prints of the memorial within hours of the dedication

Thanks to all the people of Hartland, we shall return and we hope that more will do so to visit Britain's newest war memorial.

Michael Harrison, March 2nd 2002

Katy's Nieces at the Memorial, Gill Morgan, Sue Wood and Erica Nadin-Snelling. Ceremony filmed by Crispin Sadler.

Survivors Relatives In Touch From The Memorial

Martyn Bale, Porthcawl Wales – Grandfather Alfred "Boston" Bale was 10 hours in the water after *'Glenart Castle'* sank, rescued by an American ship. Went on to live a very active life, much travelled – died aged 91.

Yvonne and Michael Griffin of Kent – Great grandfather John Roe – Stoker, able Seaman died aged 38.

Howard Burt – Great Grandson of Captain Albert Burt.

*Diver Keith Denby presents
Howard Burt (Great Grandson
of Alfred Burt Captain of
Glenart Castle) with his plate.
February 26th 2007.*

*One of the many bells was found
by divers, before and after
photographs.*

8. GALICIAN TO HMHS GLENART CASTLE

In 1900 Harland and Wolff, the renowned Belfast shipbuilders, constructed the steamship Galician on behalf of the Union Steamship Company. Following a merger the company became the Union Castle Mail Steamship Company who operated the vessel up to the time of her loss.

The ship was re-registered during WW1 as Glenart Castle as it was felt that her former name had Germanic overtones. Needing a castle name beginning with 'G', Glenart Castle was chosen. The castle from which she took her name still stands to this day situated in County Wicklow and is in business as a hotel and golf course.

As built she weighed 6576 gross registered tons. Her overall length was 430ft with a beam of 52ft 2 inches. A top speed of 12.5 knots (approx. 14mph) was achieved through coal fired boilers and steam reciprocating engines.

Glenart Castle's wartime career began in August 1914 when the German Armed Merchant Cruiser, Kaiser Wilhelm der Grosse, stopped her south of Tenerife. The captain of the German vessel would not open fire on the Glenart as she was carrying women and children; instead he sent her on her way.

Extensive service as a hospital ship followed during which time she struck a mine while on passage from France to Southampton. All 520 sick and wounded were rescued and the ship was towed to Portsmouth for extensive repairs.

Her sailing days came to an end on February 26th 1918, when she was struck by a torpedo fired by UC56 off Lundy Island, in circumstances that still anger to this day.

Today she sits upright on the seabed; unlike many modern wrecks she is still a recognisable ship, defying the years and the ferocious tides and currents. A West Country diver who visited her commented on the feeling of awe engendered by her huge steel hull. It seems to go on to infinity in the gloom where she lies, sleeping the sleep of all lost ships.

9. APPENDICES

**An extract from 'Hospital Ship Sunk – Another Red Cross Outrage'
The Times, 28th February 1918.**
    **Evidence given at the Admiralty Court of Inquiry held 27th February
1918:**

Alfred Bale (greaser) was just going on watch and had just got to the top of the ladder to the engine room when there was a loud explosion and all the lights went out. "I at once made my way along the starboard alleyway into the after well deck and then up to the boat deck to the port forward lifeboat and helped to clear and lower it. We had just got the boat into the water when I heard the chief Officer shout 'Every man for himself'. I then slid down the boats fall with two other men but before we could cast the falls adrift, the ship sank and I was thrown out of the boat. When I came to the surface I saw a boat, bottom up with 3 men clinging to it and made my way towards it and hauled myself up on the keel. Soon after I saw what I took to be a schooner coming towards us and we all shouted. A minute or two after, I saw it was not a schooner but a submarine on the surface and I said to the man next to me 'we can expect nothing from him, it is the submarine'. The submarine was not more than a 100 yds away then and I could distinctly see the outline of the hull and the conning tower. About half an hour later a raft drifted alongside and I got on board to make more room for the men on the boat. I held on to the boat for a time but had to let go. I did not see the men in the boat again." Alfred Bale was picked up from the water 10 hours later by the destroyer *U.S.S. Parker.*

Jacob Sheler was Quartermaster of the Glenart Castle and was at the wheel when the torpedo struck. At about 3am he had seen a bright light low on the starboard bow. Both he and the lookout saw it again half an hour later, now broader on the bow. The torpedo struck at 3 mins to four, in number three hatch, just abaft the engine room. The Captain ran onto the bridge, rang the engine room to stop engines and blew the ship's whistle five or six times. There was no time to use distress signals but the Captain ordered the wireless man to send out the SOS but it was never received by anyone, probably because the generators failed so quickly. The Captain said to Sheler "Now my lad, jump into the boat or you will get drowned" and went back into the chart room. Lieut. Cmdr. Burt was not seen again.

Thomas Mathews was Bosun's Mate on board the Glenart Castle. "I was just going to turn in at the time which was 5 or 6 minutes to four. I was talking to my mate about coffee and I said that it was all ready for him and then the vessel was hit. The torpedo struck us and we made for the decks. We went up on the boat deck and waited for orders. When we heard the whistle blow (steam whistle) we lowered our boats. That is the order to lower, not the station. The steam whistle being blown is the order to lower our boats. We lowered our boats and as we were lowering them the ship's stern was on the water. We just happened to shove the boat clear of the davits as she was going down, and we remained there and never moved an oar until she settled. That is all." Thomas Mathews went on to say that he saw seven lifeboats get away with people in them and two more empty ones floated off the poop. His boat remained in the neighbourhood of the sinking for about three quarters of an hour but saw nothing of the other boats. His boat contained 22 survivors, 19 crew and 3 RAMC and was landed at Swansea having been picked up by a French yawl six miles north of Lundy. Asked if there was any orders given for the Nurses to be put into the boat first he said there was not time to do anything, the ship sank in seven or eight minutes and there was no time to rescue anybody – they merely had the order to lower boats.

Thomas Casey (fireman) was turned in when the ship was struck. "I went along the alley but I had to come back again because the explosion had blown up all the after hatches – I had to return. I went up to the saloon deck. When I ran along to get to my boat station I asked the Bosun 'how is it Tom?' he said 'stand by'! He sang out asking where the sister was. He told me to stand by the after fall. Then we waited until he gave orders, and when the whistle blew we were told to lower the falls. We were told to get the boat half way down – to lower it down to the next deck. She had two decks. We lowered it down to the saloon deck to take in people. He then saw that the blocks were alright and we lowered away then. I chucked the fall clear and I went on the falls and shinned down." He saw three boats floating on the sea ahead of him on the port side. The suction of the ship sinking forced his boat away and he could not be certain if the other boats carried lights. His boat was picked up at about half past ten next morning. He concluded by saying "there was such a heavy sea running that I doubt if the other boats have lined in it".

John Hill 2nd Hand of the fishing trawler *'Swansea Castle'* gave his evidence. "We were coming into Lundy Island. When we sighted Lundy, I called the skipper and he told me to keep her in N by E and said that if I saw any lights I was to call him or when I got the light of the Lundy North Light bearing E by N. I was also to awake him if I saw any trawlers. As we were steaming along I look around with the glasses and away in the starboard rigging I saw the Hospital Ship with green lights all around her – around the saloon. She had her red side lights showing and mast-head light, and also another red light which I suppose was the Red Cross Light. We were steaming North and she was going W by N. As we were steaming along I did not know whether to alter course, but her speed took her across our head clear of us – she crossed our bow. When she got right ahead all her lights went out. When the lights went out, I turned around with the glasses in my hand to see that she went clear of us and I saw the vessel in the moonlight. Every light on board had suddenly disappeared. Of course that made me think that something was wrong and I remarked to my mate at the wheel that is was funny. Therefore, after I spoke to him, I picked up my glasses and looked around the horizon in order to see whether I could discover anything at all. As I came around with my glasses to about the NE I saw something on the water, so also did my mate, with no lights. As I looked at it, my mate said 'what is that Jack?' I said I did not know, but that is was rather funny. It looked like a Noah's Ark. After speaking to him I put the glasses down. I said a few more words and when I looked again the object had disappeared. As soon as I saw that object disappear such a thing as a submarine was far from my mind, but my mate said to me instantly 'A submarine, Jack – call the Skipper!' I shouted down to the Skipper 'Submarine, Skipper!' As soon as he got his eyes open, which was done very quickly, he said 'Over her!' I left the wheel and ran aft to call all hands to man the gun. 'Submarine' I sang out. Everyone was at his post very quickly and the gun was trained right round at once. Before I left the bridge, the Skipper said 'keep her ENE!' By going ENE it was impossible to go past that object without seeing it. As soon as I had warned everyone, I returned to the Skipper. I looked at the compass and I said to him that she was on the port bow. After I had altered her course, I said to the Skipper 'poor look-out, Skipper, she will not give us another chance'. We proceeded afterwards to Lundy".

When it got daylight they tried to signal HMT Favorita. The hospital ship had gone clean out of sight and they did not look for her. The Skipper of the 'Swansea

Castle' remarked that 'We have done our bit for the country' and although they were only just over a mile away they heard no explosion and thought that the hospital ship could not have been sunk.

Of the 186 people aboard the *'Glenart Castle'* only 31 survived. Only one boat containing 22 men was ever found and the other men were pulled from the water by the destroyer *'U.S.S. Parker'* late on the 27th.

The Times, 1918.

Excerpt from trench reports

Clive Marston Beaufoy – Army No. 309

Rank – Private, 2nd City Battalion, Royal Warwicks, B Company

7 Platoon, later commissioned 2nd Lt. 10th Royal Warwicks

Enlisted – Birmingham

Born – Columbo, Ceylon (Sri Lanka)

Resident – The Beeches (John and Ada's home), Stratford Rd., Shirley (now demolished)

Son of Samuel M and Jane Alice

Killed in Action Wednesday, 25th September 1918, aged 21 years

Memorials – Shirley War Memorial, St James Churchyard (shown as serving in 2nd City Battalion), Solihull School memorial

Roll of honour St Mary's Collegiate Church Warwick.

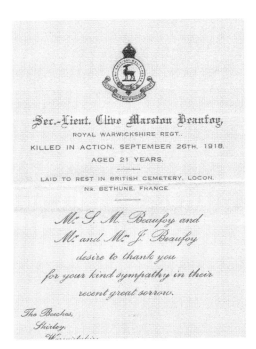

Clive Beaufoy – Front Line Log

Monday 23rd   Quiet day, LEAVE 1 O.R. proceeded on leave.

FRONT LINE
Tuesday 24th   Bn relieved 3/Worcesters on left of Brigade front. Orders
received that 3/Worcs. would repeat operations of 20th with
cooperation of this Bn. Quiet relief A & B Front line C & D
Support.
LEAVE 1 O.R. proceeded on leave.
HOSPITAL Capt H.A. Hewett admitted to Hospital.

Wednesday 25th Attack under Artillery Barrage at 8am by 3/Worcs. & Brigade
on their right. "B" Coy, 10/R.War.R. attacked at 8.30am &
after a slight repulse carried objective of LA BASSEE Rd. &
established a line beyond. "D" Coy moved up in close support.
Casualties in "B" Coy. Heavy, & line withdrawn a little. "C"
Coy moved up in support of "B" and "D".
Coy of Bn in support moved up to occupy line of resistance
vacated by our Support Coys. Line of LA BASSEE Rd not
finally established until late after much fighting. Captures 15
O.Rs.
LEAVE 2/Lt. H.L. Peskett & 1 O.R. proceed on leave.
CASUALTIES 2/Lt. C.M. Beaufoy killed.
Capt. L.R. Swinhoe & 2/Lt. A.R. Harrison wounded.
DRAFT 8 O.Rs. (all rejoining) joined Bn.

Thursday 26th   Fairly quiet. Enemy patrols repulsed.
LEAVE 2 O.R. proceeded on leave.
CASUALTY 2/Lt A.A. Chamberlain wounded.

Friday 27th   Quiet, position held & enemy counter measures Nil. Our
artillery fired on selected pints at various times to break up
concentration.

Viking Norman Origin of Beaufoy

Beaufoy/Beaufawe – old French for beautiful beech tree

The seat of this famous and ancient barony is in the neighbourhood of the Pont-L'Eveque. These Lords of Beaufou descended in the female line from Raoul, Count of Ivry, and brother of Richard I. The one who assisted in the Conquest is called Robert by William of Poitiers, and our author and Raoul in contemporary documents. He ended his days just as his two sons did, at the abbey of Bec. His descendents founded the abbey Belle Etoile and held distinguished ranks in Normandy, England and Ireland, where they seem to have formed establishments from the 12th century. The barony of Beaufoy passed to the house of Tilly, in the 14th century, and then to Harcourt, where it remains to this day. (Gwendolyn Beaufoy, Leaves From a Beech Tree, 1930 – Purchased by my Father following correspondence with Gwendolyn who contacted him seeing the notice of my birth in the papers).

Bella Fago, Galsagus (adopted in the Italian forages)
Beaufou, the most frequent early English spelling

William the Conqueror -
Father Duke Robert, mother Poppea (brother Duke Richard, grandfather Count William, great grandfather Hrolf (Rollo), great great grandfather Ragnold, first Earl of Orkney). Count William's Danish wives Esprota and Espurling. Espurling's son Raoul d'Ivry. Issue two sons, two daughters. Elder daughter married Beaufoy. Beaufoy's accompanied William in the conquest.

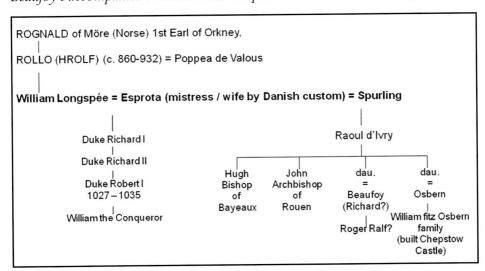

BEAUFOY PEDIGREE AND PERSONALITIES

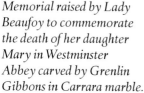

Memorial raised by Lady
Beaufoy to commemorate
the death of her daughter
Mary in Westminster
Abbey carved by Grenlin
Gibbons in Carrara marble.

The inscription:
'In a Vault
Near this Place
Lyeth the Body
of Henry Beaufoy Esq,
of Edmondscot in the
County of Warwick, Descended
of an Ancient and Noble family of
Normandy, who came
in to England at the Conquest,
He married Mary, Daughter of
Sr Walter Walker Bar
Who left three Sons
Hen: Hercules and Walter
Who lye Buried with
Him in this Vault
And four Daughters
Mary, Lucy, Martha
and Elizabeth'.

Beaufoy Memorial St. Mary's Collegiate Church, Warwick

'He had in this place a large Tomb erected by his Widow for him, that was destroyed by the Fire of Warwick, for which reason Martha his last surviving daughter at her decease did at her own charge, and desire, cause this monument and Inscription to be erected as a small remembrance of her much honoured Father. She married Sir Sam: Garth Knight Dr of Physick, and left one only daughter and heiress Beaufoy who married William Boyle Esq son to the Hon: Henry Boyle and the Right Hon: Lady Mary his Wife. Son and Daughter of the Right Hon: the Earls of Orrery; and Inchiquein of the Kingdom of Ireland.

Edmonscote – Old Beaufoy Manor. Guide Dogs for the Blind Association. Midlands Regional Training Centre. We are very grateful to them for the interest and care they have taken of Edmondscote Manor, the last of the Beaufoy Manorial Holdings and the history they have kept alive there.

Sources of Information: *Family Research:* Doreen Agutter, BA Genealogist; Dinah Pickard, family research; Peter Platt, e-family research. *Research:* Michael Harrison, MA History; Deborah Sullivan, MA.

Bronze plaques, approximately 3 inches in diameter, with each casualty's name cast into the surface, were sent to next of kin (see page 141).

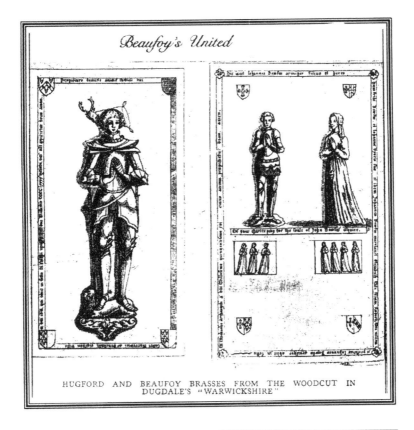

HUGFORD AND BEAUFOY BRASSES FROM THE WOODCUT IN DUGDALE'S "WARWICKSHIRE"

A Beaufoy was Chancellor to the Exchequer in Normandy prior to the Conquest, Beaufoy's (Roger and Ralf) came over in the Conquest, William Beaufoy, made Bishop of Thetford 1086.

Family given many holdings in various southern counties. Plaque in Norwich Cathedral to Archdeacon Beaufoy. There are records of Baron holdings; Norfolk/Lincoln/Rutland/Oxford from then to 14th Century. Sheriffs in Lincoln, Knights in Rutland.

Henry II Bride Sale (raising money):

Listed in 1186 Alice de Beaufoe and son Thomas age 2 (Sir Thomas Beaufoy of Rutland died 1185).

Waterperry Holdings Oxfordshire from 1115. Brass Plaque Isabell Beaufo, Waterperry Church (1370). Warwickshire holdings acquired on marriage of Beaufoy and Hugford 1440. Beaufoy Vault in St Mary's Collegiate Church Warwick destroyed by great fire of Warwick 1694. Hugford and Beaufoy brasses in Warwickshire 1445, recorded by William Dougdale in history of Warwickshire. Sir Thomas of Edmondscote and Guys Cliff Knighted by King James. His son Henry Knighted by King Charles II in the bedchamber (died without heirs 1664). Estates sold circa 1670.

Replacement Memorial at St Mary's Collegiate Church, Warwick, South Aisle; with history of family. Memorial to Henry's daughter erected in Westminster Abbey.

Beaufoy family from Sir Thomas established in Meriden – from this branch all present Beaufoys traced back worldwide.

Quaker religion adopted by many, Mark Beaufoy corn oil miller – learned vinegar brewery skills in Holland, set up large brewing factory of wine, vinegar and ginger beer in Lambeth in 1730. Painted by Gainsborough, destroyed in the blitz 1942. Mark stopped brewing gin after seeing the Hogarth paintings of depravity caused by cheap gin sales.

A son Henry Beaufoy MP spoke against slavery – visited slave ship in the Thames, gave up Quakerism to become an MP.

Quaker ethos, Henry's wife Elizabeth (nee Jenks) started a Ragged School under the railway arches in Lambeth; they opened a

Mark Beaufoy, aged 62, 1781, Painted by Gainsborough.

Henry Beaufoy, MP, died 1795
Painted by Gainsborough.

Mrs Henry Beaufoy,
Painted by Gainsborough.

building close by for the education of illiterate and unemployed boys. This was later transferred to a purpose built building, the Beaufoy Institute, Black Prince Road a large spacious airy building, with machinery installed. Henry also gave a £10,000 donation to the City of London School. His father Mark gave an annual silver medal for mathematics which was carried on by Henry to the present day as a bronze medal, an annual Beaufoy Day is still held.

Henry Benjamin Hanbury
Beaufoy, F.R.S. From the
original picture painted for the
City of London School, 1845
By Pickersgill.

Henry Benjamin Hanbury Beaufoy – Fellow of Royal Society, nautical and hydraulic experiments. First Englishman to climb Mont Blanc. Beaufoy Heads of Household: 1881 Census, 27, heads of households usually male at this time.

Gwendolyn Beaufoy published Beaufoy History 'Leaves of a Beech Tree' 1930 from the Beaufoy papers she had inherited.

Beaufoy factory, Lambeth joined up to form British Vinegars, destroyed by bombing with the death of Managing Director, George Maurice Beaufoy 1941. Beaufoy Institute used until 1947,

Principle Stone laid by Mildred Scott Beaufoy, wife of Mark Hanbury Beaufoy J.P. 21st February 1907. "Those that do teach young babes do it with gentle means and easy tasks".

2012 land eventually cleared and sold with the listed Beaufoy Institute for £9.4m. A million is being given to the London Community Foundation for charitable purposes. The Beaufoy Institute bought by the Diamond Way Tibetan/Buddhist head, Dalai Lama. The Beaufoy dedication plaque remains outside the Institute and the Diamond Way are creating a memorial room to the Beaufoy founders – continuing the Beaufoy ethos!

Beaufoys Today
Sue Elphick, MBE for charitable services to the Countess of Chester Hospital NHS Trust, Chester.

Guy Beaufoy, ecologist, on the board of directors for European Forum on Nature Conservation and Pastoralism (EFNCP).

Simon Beaufoy, screenwriter, The Full Monty, Slum Dog Millionaire, Salmon Fishing in the Yemen, etc. OSCAR and BAFTA awards.

THE LONDON DIAMOND

Saturday 5 April 2014 marked an important day in the history of Buddhism in London and the UK. After over a year of renovation works to prepare the Beaufoy Institute to host a regular programme of meditation and events, the London Diamond Way Buddhist Centre officially opened its doors to the public.

Under bright sunshine, a red carpet was rolled out above the freshly scrubbed steps of the Buddhist centre. Black Prince Road held an eager crowd of visitors who had arrived early. From midday, hundreds of guests streamed in for the ceremony, including many special guests from the local community, interfaith representatives and locally elected councillors. Delegates from other Buddhist organisations attended, including Dechen, the Buddhist Society, ALBA, Buddhist Community Centre UK, the Buddhist Chaplaincy Support Group, and the Lumbini Nepali Buddha Dharma Society. Dr Sunil Kariyakarawana, the Buddhist Chaplain to Her Majesty's Armed Forces was one of the special guests, and Venerable Simon Gates, Archdeacon of Lambeth, kindly attended on behalf of the Bishop of Southwark.

Erica Beaufoy, Jigme Rinpoche, Lama Ole Nydahl and Councillor Paul McGlone, cutting the ribbon to open the London Diamond Way Buddhist Centre at the Beaufoy, 5 April 2014.

MEMORIALS

KATY'S PARENTS'
HEADSTONE,
SUTTON COLDFIELD,
WARWICKSHIRE.

HOLLYBROOK MEMORIAL, SOUTHAMPTON.

HARTLAND POINT: inscription reads as follows:

*IN PROUD AND GRATEFUL MEMORY
OF THOSE WHO GAVE THEIR LIVES
IN THE HOSPITAL SHIP
GLENART CASTLE
PLEASE REMEMBER MASTER LT. CMDR.
BURT. MATRON KATY BEAUFOY THE SHIP'S
OFFICERS, CREW AND MEDICAL STAFF
WHO DIED WHEN THEIR SHIP WAS
TORPEDOED BY UC 56 IN THE EARLY
HOURS OF 26TH FEB 1918 THE SHIP LIES 20
MILES WNW FROM THIS STONE FOR
THOSE IN PERIL ON THE SEA
R.I.P.
DEDICATED 26.02.2002*

YORK MINSTER:

Memorial to Women who died on active service during the Great War. WAR MEMORIAL, CHURCH OF ST. JAMES, SHIRLEY, SOLIHULL: This memorial has the Ship's name carved after that of Katy. Her nephew, Clive Marston Beaufoy, is also recorded here. Clive Marston Beaufoy in St Mary's Collegiate Church Warwick Roll of Honour 1914-1918.

10. INDEX OF PEOPLE

SURNAME	FIRST NAME	TITLE	ORGANISATION/ RELATIONSHIP
Acton		Matron	
Adams	Edie		
Allan		Lt	
Allen		Mr	
Anderson		Cpt	
Ansell	H	Mr	
Ashford	J	Mr	
Barfield			RAMC
Barnish		Lt	
Barton		Matron	
Beaufoy	Ada	Mrs	married to John & sister in law to Katy.
Beaufoy	Clive		nephew to Katy.
Beaufoy	Joe	Mr	brother to Katy.
Beaufoy	John	Mr	brother to Katy.
Beaufoy	Louie	Mrs	married to Joe & sister in law to Katy.
Beaufoy	Sam		brother to Katy, father to Clive.
Beavan		Orderly	
Beedon-Smith		Matron	
Bell		Dr	Australian
Bennett		Cpt	
Bicker		Cptn (Dr)	
Bickham		Sister	
Bilton		Sister	
Birkett		Sister	
Blakely		Matron	
Bodey(ie)	May	Sister	
Bond		Matron	
Brown		Sister	
Brown		Lt	
Burleigh		Mrs	BRCS
Butler	SG	Sister	
Butler		Lt	
Caine		Cpt	
Camplin		Mr & Mrs	
Carnaevon		Lady	
Cavanagh		Sister	
Chandler		Mr & Mrs	
Chapman		Sister	
Clarke		Sister	
Clayton-Smith		Matron	
Clewes		Cpt	
Coad		Cpt	
Collins		Staff Major	

SURNAME	FIRST NAME	TITLE	ORGANISATION/ RELATIONSHIP
Collyer		Sister	
Condick		Sister	
Cooper		Sister	
Cornwell		Sister	
Coule-Kneale		Dr	
Courthall-Thompson		Col	BRCS Commissioner
Cruise		Miss	VAD
Culverwell		Cpt	
Cumpton		Minister	Presbyterian
Darton	Nora	Mrs	
Davidson		Cpt	
Davis		Padre	C of E
Dick		Mr	RNPF
Dickinson		Lt	
Dickson		Mrs	
Doherty		Mr	
Dowding		Sister	
Dowding		Senior Chaplain Col	
Drake		Mr	
Duff		Col	CRAMC
Duget		Lt	RN Res
Earle		Sister	
Emmerson		Col	
Evans		Dr	
Falkner		Sister	New Zealand
Ferguson		Col	
Flewitt		Cpt	
Flewitt		Mrs	
Flewitt		Teddy	
Foley		Sister	
Fordham		Miss	
Foster		Sister	
Freestone		Cpt	Chaplain to 38th General Hospital
Galbraith		Sister	
Ganad		Lt	
Garrad		Lt	
Gilharn		Sister	
Gillis		Cpt	
Goldstraw		Sister	
Goodfellow	A	Pte	
Goodyear		Mr	
Gordon-Mitchell		Lt	
Gough			
Grant		Mr	RCC
Green		Miss	
Grenville		Mr	
Grenville		Mrs	
Grierson		Matron	
Griffiths		Sister	
Guilbride		Sister	Canadian
Gumner		Lt	
Gunson		Mr	
Hall		Matron	
Harley		Mr	

SURNAME	FIRST NAME	TITLE	ORGANISATION/ RELATIONSHIP
Harries		Matron	
Harris		Mr	
Hawken		Sister	New Zealand
Hayne	Nellie	Mrs	
Hebbert		Sister	
Hemsley		Purser	
Henderson	B	Sister	
Henry		Cpt	
Hoadley		Matron	
Hobbes		Sister	
Hodgins		Sister	
Holcroft		Miss	
Hollows		Sister	
Hopkins		Mrs	
Hughes		Sister	
Hughes		Mrs	
Humfries		Sister	
Hunter		Cpt	
Hynes		Mrs	
Jackson		Mr	
Jackson		Mrs	
.lardin		Sister	
Jenkins		Cpt	
Jentell		Nurse	
Johnson		Mrs	
Jones	Beatrice	Matron	
Joyce			VAD
Keen		Sister	
Kent		Mr	
Kenworthy		Mr	
King		Lt	
Kirk		Sister	
Kirk	Nellie		married to Howard & sister to Katy.
Kirk	Howard		brother in law to Katy.
Kirk	Kath		daughter of Howard & Nellie.
Kirk	Dorrington		son of Howard & Nellie.
Kneale	Dr		
Kneale	Kath	Mrs	
Lauertine		Cpt	
Lawlers		Cpt	
Lefebre	M		BRCS Commissioner
Levd		Miss	
Lewis		Col	
Linklala		Chief Officer	
Lorrimer		Mr	
Macfarlane		Matron	
MacMakon	Henry	Sir	
MacMakon		Lady	
Maitland		Mr	
Martin		Major	
Maskell	C	Sister	
Mayo Robson		Col Sir	
McCarthy		Matron	
McDonald		Stoker	

SURNAME	FIRST NAME	TITLE	ORGANISATION/ RELATIONSHIP
McInnes	Rev	Bishop of Jerusalem	
McKenzie		Dr	
Melrose		Dr	
Metheun	Paul Sandford	Lord	Governor of Malta when Katy was there
Metheun		Lady	
Michckophilaus		Mr & Mrs	"Greek Protestant Minister"
Miles		Cpt	
Miller		Sister	New Zealand
Miller		Cpt	
Mitchell		Matron	
Molson		Miss	BRCS
Morrish		Cptn (Dr)	
Mudie		Lt	
Mullen		Sister	
Murphy	J	Matron	
Nobb		Mr (MO)	
O'Pearson		Sister	
O'Riordan	S	Sister	
Oakley		Sister	
Oclay	Rice		
Oram		Matron	
Osborne		Sister	
Osbourne		Matron	
Palin		Sister	
Parkes		Mrs	VAD
Parkinson		Mrs	
Pemberthy		Major	
Penbertly		Cpt	
Phillips		Padre	C of E
Phipps		Miss	
Pollard		Dr	
Pollard		Mrs	
Porter	James	General Sir	
Prendergast		Padre	
Prince		Lt	
Puller		Mrs	
Rabington		Miss	
Radcliffe		Miss	VAD
Ravenhill		Dr	
Reid		Lt	
Remberthy		Cpt	
Richmond		Mrs	BRCS
Richmond		Cpt	
Richmond		Mrs	
Rigby		Chaplain RC	
Riley		Sister	
Roskell		Mrs	VAD
Rothwell		Sister	
Rudd		Mr	
Ruffers		Mrs	
Sale	Edith		
Sale	Dolly		
Salt	D		
Samson		Wing Commander	

SURNAME	FIRST NAME	TITLE	ORGANISATION/ RELATIONSHIP
Scott		Major	
Sellar		Major	
Showells		Mrs	
Sinclair		Matron	
Smith		Sister	
Smith	LG		
Smith	Dennis		
Snell		Miss	
Sorrie		Sister	
Staverly		Cpt	
Stephenson		Mr	
Stephenson		Mrs	
Stockwell		Cpt	
Stuart		Sister	
Stuart	MS	Sister	
Sutton		Colonel	DDMS
Tallis	Walter		
Tatum		Dr	
Taylor		Miss	VAD
Thomas		Dr	PMO
Thomas	H	Sister	
Thomas	NG	Sister	
Thomson		Sister	
Thomson	ME	Miss	
Thorne	May	Miss	
Thursby	Cecil	Admiral Sir	
Tompkins		Staff Nurse	
Turner		Lt Com	
Twinning		Mr	
Tyndall/Tindall		Sister	
Waca		Mr	
Wai		Chaplain RC	
Waldron		Mrs	
Warner	M	Rev	
Washer		Cptn (Dr)	
Watchlin		Cpt	
Watney		Miss	
Watson		Mrs	
Westland		Miss	BRCS
White		Orderly	
Wilcox		Padre	C of E
Wilford		Cpt	
Wilkinson		Mrs	
Williams		Cpt	
Willoughby	Bertha	Matron	
Wilson		Matron	
Woodford		Staff Nurse	
Woolett		Major	
Worth	Charles	Major	
Yeo		General	

11. INDEX OF SHIPS

HMS Adamant	Submarine Depot Ship, launched in 1911.
SS Andania	Cunard Line (Troop Transport), launched 1913, torpedoed 1918 off North Coast of Ireland.
RMS Aquitania	Cunard Line, nicknamed 'Ship Beautiful'. Launched 1913. Used as Hospital Ship in the Dardanelles 1915.
SS Aragon	Royal Mail Liner used as a headquarters ship.
SS Arcadian	Cunard Liner used as a troop transport. Torpedoed off Marseilles.
HMHS Arturias	Hospital Ship.
SS Assaye	Hospital Ship, P&O Line.
Asturias	Hospital Ship.
Auralia	Hospital Ship.
SS Avoca	A British India Liner used as a hospital ship.
RMS Baltania	Royal Mail Liner used as a hospital ship, launched 1909.
Ben-ma-Cree	
Beri-Beri	Sloop.
SS Braemar Castle	Union Castle Line, used as a troop ship.
HMHS Britannic	Hospital Ship. Sister ship to Titanic, White Star Line. Probably mined 21st November 1916, 40 miles south east of Athens.
SS Caledonia	Anchor Line, used as troop transport.
HMS Camelion	Acorn Class Destroyer, launched 1910.
SS Cameronian	Cunard Line, used as troop transport.
Carnac	
SS Cashmine	Transport Ship.
SS City of Birmingham	Ellerman line Passenger Ship used as troop transport.
Comet	Acorn Class Torpedo Boat Destroyer sunk in 1918.
HMS Cornwallis	Duncan Class launched 1906. Sunk off Malta 9th January 1917 by U32.
SS Delta	New Zealand Hospital Ship.
SS Devanha	Hospital Ship.
SS Dongola	Hospital Ship, P&O Line.
HMS Doris	Eclipse Class Cruiser, launched 1896, sold for scrap 1919.
HMHS Dover Castle	Union Castle Line Hospital Ship, sunk 26th May 1917 by U67.
HMHS Dunluce Castle	Union Castle Line Hospital Ship, launched 1904.
Dwana	
E 14	E Class Submarine, launched July 1914, mined off the Dardanelles on 22nd January 1918.
Endymion	Hospital Ship, Edgar Class large cruiser launched 1891, broken up March 1921.

HMHS Essequibo	Hospital Ship.
SS Etac	Sheer Line Paraffin boat with a Chinese crew.
SS Evani	South African Hospital Ship.
SS Formosa	
HMS Foxhound	Torpedo Boat Destroyer, 'G' Class launched 1909.
HMT Franconia	Cunard Line, used as troop transport, launched 1911, torpedoed in 1916.
HMHS Galeka	Union Castle Line Hospital Ship, mined Cape le Hagie October 1916.
HMHS Glenart Castle	Union Castle Line Hospital Ship.
HMHS Glengorran Castle	Hospital Ship. Formally German, launched 1898, converted to Hospital Ship during WW1, scrapped 1930.
HMHS Gloucester Castle	Union Castle Line Hospital Ship, launched 1911.
SS Gondola	Hospital Ship.
SS Gondrea	
SS Goorkha	Union Castle Line Hospital Ship.
SS Grantully Castle	Union Castle Line Hospital Ship, launched 1909.
SS Guildford Castle	Union Castle Line Hospital Ship, launched 1911.
SS Haverford	American Line Troop Ship. Launched 1901, damaged 1917, scrapped 1925.
HMHS Herefordshire	Hospital Ship.
HMTS Hiberinia	Troop Ship.
SS Hunt's Green	
SS Huntsend	German boat taken over by Union Castle Lines.
SS Ionian	Allan Line Troop Ship.
SS Isonzo	
SS Ivernia	Cunard Line Troop Transport, launched 1899, torpedoed by a German submarine 31st December 1916.
HMS Jonquil	Flower Class Minesweeper, launched 1915.
SS Karapara	
HMT Knight Errant	Troop Ship.
SS La France	French Liner used as a Hospital Ship.
SS Landovery Castle	Union Castle Line, sunk by U86 116 miles from
Fastnet Rock	
HMHS Lanfranc	Booth Line Hospital Ship, launched 1906, torpedoed 17th April 1917.
SS Letitia	
HMS Lord Nelson	Pre-Dreadnought battleship, launched 1906.
SS Magdolena	Royal Mail Line, launched 1889, served as a troop ship.
SS Marcain Kenworthy	
HMS Marguerite	An 'Arabis' class sloop, launched 1915.
HM Marquette	Transport Ship. Launched 1897 as Bodicea. Sold 1898 to Atlantic Transport Line, re-named and chartered to Red Star Line.
RMS Mauritania	
SS Minnetonka	
SS Minnewoska	Red Star Line.
SS Mitra	Oil Steamer.

SS Neuralia	Hospital Ship.
SS Nile	
SS Northland	
SS Orient	
RMS Orsova	Orient Line.
SS Osouza	P&O Line.
SS Panama	Hospital Ship, Panama Steam Ship Company.
SS Persia	Torpedoed 1st January 1916.
PS Queen Victoria	Isle of Man Paddle Steamer.
HS Rasheed	Hospital Ship.
TBD Redpole	Torpedo Boat Destroyer Acorn Class, launched 1910.
HMHS Reiva	Hospital Ship.
SS Royal Edward	Troop Ship, formerly called the Cairo by Canadian Northern Steam Ship Company. Torpedoed by UB14 13th August 1915.
SS Salicia	
HMHS Salta	Hospital Ship sunk off Le Havre 10th April 1917.
SS Scotian	
SS Simla	
Smoke	Russian Cruiser.
HMHS Somali	Naval Hospital Ship.
SS Southland	Torpedoed en route to Gallipoli.
SS Sphinx	French Hospital Ship.
St George	Edgar Class Cruiser, launched 1892, scrapped 1920.
St Margaret of Scotland	Hospital Ship.
HMHS Soudan	P&O Line.
SS Thelirius	
HMHS Triad	Hospital Ship.
HMT Tunisian	Troop Ship.
U13	Launched 1910, sunk North Sea Sept 14th 1914.
SS Valdivia	Hospital Ship.
SS Venezuelos	
SS Victoria	P&O Line.
Ville de Rouen	Le Havre.
HMHS Wandila	Hospital Ship.
HMAT Warilda	Australian Transport Ship run by Adelaide Steam Ship Company, torpedoed and sunk 13th August 1918 in the English Channel.

12. ABBREVIATIONS

Alex	Alexandria
AOD	Army Ordnance Department
Arrd	Arrived
ASC	Army Service Corps
Bkft	Breakfast
BRCS/Red X	British Red Cross Society
CAMC	Canadian Army Medical Corps
DC	Dover Castle
DDMS	Deputy Director Medical Services
Dip	Diphtheria
Gen Hosp/G.H	General Hospital
HMHS	His Majesty's Hospital Ship
HMT	His Majesty's Transport
Hosp	Hospital
Inj	Injection
Junc	Junction
MO	Medical Officer
NZAMC	New Zealand Army Medical Corps
Ord	Orderlies
Para-ty	Para-typhoid
PM	Principal Matron
PMO	Principal Medical Officer
Pts	Patients
QAIMNSR	Queen Alexandra's Imperial Military Nursing Service Reserve
Qrtrs	Quarters
RAMC	Royal Army Medical Corps
RCC	Roman Catholic Chaplain
Recd	Received
Retd	Returned
S.A	South Africa
Sal/Sala	Salonika
Sr	Sister
TBD	Torpedo Boat Destroyer
VAD	Volunteer Aid Detachment
WO	Warrant Officer
(...?...)	Space left in diary for unknown name

ACKNOWLEDGEMENTS

How to get to know your relations? Find you have been hoarding gold in the form of an old family diary and you discover cousins you never knew as children. This is how Great Auntie Katy's Diary has drawn together branches of the Beaufoy family tree. I had inherited her diary together with most of her medals and Dead Man's Penny, some family photographs and archive documents including the War Office telegram and letter of condolence from the King and Queen: Erica Nadin-Snelling a wealth of genealogical data and a great fascination with our family history: Claire Burley inherited some more photographs and the medal awarded to Katy by the Italian Queen between her service in the 2nd Boer War and the 1914-1918 War, and Gill Morgan couldn't put down the original brittle closely written loose note book pages, so closely written that some could only be deciphered with a magnifying glass, until it was transcribed on to safer paper.

Between us we have brought together not only the facts for this part of the book but have widened our knowledge through others with differing but connected interests, drawing together different branches of the family – the branches of a beech tree – the origin of the name Beaufoy.

This story includes Katy Beaufoy's diary from May 10th 1915 to September 16th 1917, a fascinating account of her service as Sister and Matron in the Great War. The diary has been faithfully reproduced with abbreviations and spellings as written, gaps where she meant to add a name but never had the time, and part text-July-September 1916 where pages were torn. It was originally transcribed with help from family and friends by her great niece Gillian Morgan.

Outside the family group we owe an immense debt of gratitude to Michael and Joyce Harrison without whom you would not be reading this document. We cannot thank them enough for all their time, knowledge, research and skills that they, alongside Claire Harrison, Mark & Lynette Bentley, Douglas & Ann Rudhen have brought into facilitating its production. As a family we have also been supported by the skill and enthusiasm of Keith Denby from the Ilfracombe

Sub Aqua Club whose discovery of the Glenart Castle wreck (Auntie Katy's final resting place) became a fitting ending to the collation of all our efforts.

Sue Wood, Warwick – December 2006

Thanks to Sue Wood nee Kirk, great niece of Katy Beaufoy, who lent me the original diary. This had been saved, with all Katy's medals and 'Dead Woman's Penny'*, by Sue's father, Dorrington Kirk.

Grateful thanks to Claire Harrison, Mark & Lynette Bentley and Douglas & Ann Rodham – the "Computer Whizz Kids" who typed, twitched and sorted the text, arranged photographs and included drawings as drawn by Katy.

Keeping the best till last without Joyce & Michael Harrison you would not be reading this book. We cannot thank them enough for all the time, knowledge and skills they have contributed. Michael and Joyce have spent hours on research confirming details to facilitate this book.

I am so humbled and thrilled by all their expertise and to hold this printed diary is as exciting as the birth of my first child.

Gill Morgan

My Cousin Gill has been the motivating force and continuing thread behind this book her visit to Clive's grave, the scene of the ship wreck, the erection of the memorial on headland point, the superb annual service of dedication to the ship at the memorial and subsequent annual service on February 26th with her recruiting of Michael and Joyce and inspiring my daughter Deborah Sullivan and myself to be proud to publish this book in memory of our Great Aunt Katy.

Gwendolyn Beaufoy, who inherited the family papers and published privately *Leaves From A Beech Tree*, in 1930, corresponded with my family (letters kept) at the notice of my birth and wanted to know our connection with the family. Doreen, whose family married into the Beaufoy's in the 1600s. We are grateful for her specialised knowledge, including the connection of Raol d'Ivry. Dinah Pickhard – a Beaufoy granddaughter – the hours that she has spent in the county records office, and compilation of a huge lineage. Peter Platt's electronic format of each family to three generations, and research into Wills.

Erica Nadin-Snelling (née Beaufoy)

Front Cover Detail

The front cover photographs shows the British Hospital ship *Glenart Castle*, Katy on a camel when visiting Egypt, and Katy in uniform; this photograph appeared on the front page of the *Daily Sketch* shortly after the ship's sinking.